Zilosophy on Golf

Observations on the parallels between life and golf

Michael A. Zildjian

Edited by Jason Ronstadt

Published by Zilosophy

Zilosophy Books
An imprint of Zilosophy LLC
www.Zilosophy.org

Book cover design © Luis Torres
Book Interior & Ebook design by Soumi Goswami
Logo/ Branding © Kelly K., kkz/cbbo
Z bio photo and back cover photo © Ani Lee Zildjian
Photograph wardrobe provided by Haus of Grey/ Matte Grey

Zilosophy books may be purchased for resale by contacting
info@zilosophy.org for more information.

A portion of proceeds from all book sales is donated
to youth golf initiatives.

First Edition
Printed in The United States of America

LCCN- 2018905595
ISBN – 978-0-692-12052-1

Zilosophy on Golf
Course Layout

i.   *Fore! Word by Jason Gore* vii

ii. *Introduction - The Driving Range.* 1

• Hole 1   Swing Your Swing. 9

• Hole 2   Practice Doesn't Make Perfect. 19

• Hole 3   Confidence Is Key. 29

• Hole 4   Mind Games 37

• Hole 5   Re:Vision 47

• Hole 6   The Moment Of Impact 57

• Hole 7   Play It As It Lies 67

• Hole 8   Grinding And Thriving. 77

• Hole 9   Lost And Found. 87

• Making The Turn   Front 9 Review/ Score 96

• Hole 10   Timing Is Everything. 99

• Hole 11   Body Of Work. 107

• Hole 12   Jerk. Off. 115

• Hole 13   Integri-tee. 123

• Hole 14   Inclusivi-tee 131

• Hole 15   Not So Great Expectations 141

• Hole 16   Critic's Choice 149

• Hole 17   Lesson...The Pain. 159

- Hole 18   Enjoy The Journey 169
- The Scorer's Tent   Back 9 Review/ Total Score 176

iii. *The 19th Hole* 178
iv. *Acknowledgements* 180
v. *Z Bio* 184

Scott,

Timing is everything!

M.G.3

Scott,

Timing is everything!

[signature]

Fore! Word
by Jason Gore

As I sit here in my hotel room, again, I ponder where I'm going with this crazy game, and this even crazier life. I am one of the truly lucky people in the world. I have a wife and family that I absolutely adore, and a career that has been somewhat fruitful. I can look back on my career and wish I would have done a few things differently, but not many. I've met some incredible people along the way. From Presidents to part-time gardeners. All wonderful and fascinating people. I've got trophies and a bad back to show for this career.

There are certain things that I wish I would have found when I was younger. One of them is this book. This book has shown me that we make this game, which I think is a microcosm of life, way more difficult than it needs to be. The first time I read this book, I realized that this is not a book for professional golfers, but for every golfer. Better yet, every person.

Michael Zildjian (or as I call him "Z") has been a close friend since 1994. We met at Pepperdine University in this little town called Malibu, California. I say that with sarcasm, because it's possibly one of the prettiest places in the world. But, I digress. Z was one of the first people I met at Pepperdine. He was a good friend of my roommate and we immediately hit it off. We see eye-to-eye. We've been close friends ever since, but I never knew he had this in him. He wrote something that I've been waiting for my entire career, let alone life.

When I read this book for the first time, I was a little reluctant. I knew Z had some deep thoughts, but I was never expecting him to put them into words, or on paper. This book fits perfectly with the game. I love the fact that I can go through it over and over and read the chapters that I feel I'm lacking in. I get something new and different every time. I learn something new about myself every time I look back and refresh.

This is not a book that talks down to you. This is a book that walks with you. Through every agony. Through every glory. It's all in there. I never feel alone when I read through it. I feel like we are walking through this together. Z shares triumphs and defeats. Just like you and I go through. This book is about being imperfect at a perfect game. It prepares you to play your best golf by realizing that we aren't perfect and that sweet spot of the clubface is elusive. But, it's okay. The book is about mentally preparing to hit the perfect shot. It's about being in the right frame of mind and focused to be the best you can be. Not for the day. For that particular shot. That moment. It's about being in the moment of the most important shot of your life. The one you are about to hit. You can't change the past and you certainly can't control the future. You can only control your thoughts about the shot you are hitting right now. Eliminating the distractions. Clearing the mind. Not worrying about that tee shot with the water on the 13th hole when you are standing over a 4-footer for par on hole six. We all do it. Even the best have done it. We are human. It happens. But, with the help of this book, we can change that way of thinking. We can learn to be and live in the moment. Not worry about that random gust of wind that might take that purely struck shot offline and plug it into the bunker. Accept it and move on. You've done all you can. And with this book, you can see and accept this in ways that you've never even thought about before.

Z has a lot of life experience that he uses to relate all that he has done, and then takes it to the first tee. It's life's little lessons that are so meaningful to golf.

One afternoon, after playing a round of golf at Lakeside Golf Club in Toluca Lake, CA, a friend of mine came up to me at the table, looked right at me and said, "How's your confidence?" He said it in a way that only this guy could say it. In his thick New Jersey accent, he explained to me what Tiger Woods and John Daly said to him about what they think after they hit a bad shot. In so many words, he told me that both of them say it bothers them, but they don't dwell on it because "they are pros, they can handle anything." He then proceeded to hand me this little yellow Post-It note that said, "Enjoy what fate sends your way. Don't dread it." Basically, there is nothing on the golf course that I can't handle. It doesn't matter what you did, it matters what you do from here. The exact same principle as this book. That guy on the golf course was actor, Joe Pesci. I asked him if he was sure that he wanted to give it to me. He said, "Yeah I'll just make another one." Haha! Perfect Pesci moment. It was almost like he was playing a character out of a movie. Being the head boss in one of his gangster movies. But, it hit home. And, just like this book, he was right!

By following this book, going back to reference chapters, you will play better golf. I have found the fun again in playing the game that I have always loved. For a while, it became a business. Zilosophy helped me realize why I love the game. It simplified the process and helped me understand that I'm not alone. We all go through this! Whether you are playing for 50 cents against your buddies, or trying to win the U.S. Open, it's all perspective. Enjoy this book and love the game!

— JG

Introduction
(The Driving Range)

*"You have to play by the rules of golf just like you have
to live by the rules of life. There's no other way."*
— *Babe Didrickson*

This great game of golf has been a passion of mine since the late 1980's, and playing golf has helped me to better understand my life beyond the links. So, if you are willing to forgive me the indulgence of talking about myself, I will promise not to abuse your patience as I share some of the insights that the game has seen fit to bestow upon me. I do not claim to possess the skill of Ben Hogan, and I cannot promise you the wisdom of Ben Franklin. You may also be relieved to learn that I am not a professional therapist.

Years ago, I had a successful career in the music business, a great bachelor pad in the Hollywood Hills, and I traveled a lot while hobnobbing with rock stars and celebrities. It was a lot of fun, but something was missing. Something big. I spent a lot of my time building egos and bank accounts, but I needed to find a way to do something else. I wasn't sure what to do but I knew that I needed to spend more time helping others. I had always been good at guiding my family and friends through the challenges they faced. But how the heck was I going to turn that into a career? Go back to school to become a therapist? No thanks. That didn't feel right for me.

Like many people on a spiritual journey, I was searching for answers to the big questions. So, I did what many Angelinos do. I threw some clothes into the backseat of my car and headed for Sedona, AZ. Out there in the open air I hoped that the Universe would give me some direction. And it did. The second night I was there I began writing. I had never felt this way before. The thoughts and ideas were pouring out of me. I kept writing, and by the end, I realized that although I hadn't previously written anything other than business proposals and marketing plans, I might actually have something to offer if I could help by providing some useful perspectives on life. Suddenly it hit me that I was a pretty decent public speaker, as well. Maybe I could write books and then go speak to people about them? It sounded great but I had no idea how to do it.

I mean who am I to write a book about life when I clearly don't have it all figured out? Then again, maybe that's the point. I can write and speak as someone who is on the front lines with everyone else searching to find a way to unveil the best version of myself. Rather than someone who stands on a stage with a giant fake smile telling you that I have all the answers, maybe it's more important to be right there with you simply asking questions that allow us all to find our own answers. In this way, maybe I could be a catalyst for a real conversation.

The complete tale of how I figured out how to recreate myself is another story for another time. What was important about my trip to Sedona was that it helped me see that by examining the parallels between life and golf, I might be able to help readers discover the best version of themselves – and help myself in the process.

As I incorporated notes from friends and mentors, I was challenged to dive deep into each chapter and truly reckon with each concept. The writing process was challenging and equally rewarding, because I was trying to master these concept as I wrote about them.

When I took the time to give myself a score from each chapter I really started to see personal gains. I identified and addressed some key areas that really needed more attention and commitment. I knew the book could be useful to others because it was already helping me, and it has continued to remind me to strive to be my best at all times no matter what is occurring around me.

So why did I choose golf for the first book in this series? One night not too long after Sedona, I had a dream about seeing the shot before you hit it, committing completely to the brief moment of impact and then letting go of attachment to outcome and allowing the ball to go where it goes. A couple of days later while playing a round of golf I focused on nothing but those 3 things. On the 3rd hole, I missed a hole-in-one by inches, and I knew right then that, I had enough to start a book.

Additionally, golf like many other seemingly trivial activities, can be a great mirror of life, if we are willing to see our own reflection. If you tend to overthink, are often filled with anxiety, or run short on patience – if you are hard on yourself or suffer from a lack of joy in your golf game – then it is likely that those same things are adversely affecting your life off the course as well. If any of this sounds familiar, remember that you're not alone and there is hope.

This book is meant to be a guide. It is an exploration of parallels between life and golf. It aims to bring awareness through the exploration of clear concepts that ask the reader to push and strive for mastery. This is not meant to be gospel and I, in no way, make any claims that I am perfect or 'have it all figured out' in life, and certainly not in golf. I hope that you will enjoy reading the stories, but also that you will use it as a reference to help you prioritize what is most important (to you) both on and off of the course.

Most of us have had the experience of having a smooth warm-up session on the range where we feel comfortable and hit the ball really well. It's only minutes later that we then find ourselves on the first tee box, our major anxiety setting in and suddenly we feel like a completely different golfer. One of the hardest things in golf is to bring your confidence from the range onto the course. To swing freely when it counts the most. It's no different in life. Discussing these concepts and changes can seem simple in theory. It's another story when we actually have to implement change in reality. One thing that I've learned about human beings is that we see that 'aha' moment about something that will spark us to find a heightened state. This moment can be exhilarating, but all too often we revert back to our less productive comfort zone. It takes incredible faith and commitment to turn these moments of clarity into our new normal.

No matter what you want to do in life, your goals will require consciousness and commitment. And then there's a bunch of other stuff that we have very little power over. What I am offering here is a chance to reflect on taking ownership of what you can control and letting go of the things you cannot control, through patience and acceptance.

This is not a self-help book, regardless of the section where you found it. You don't need help. There is nothing wrong with you. As human beings we are all imperfect. It is however, a self-awareness book. We all need awareness in order to attempt to bring our best to our games and our lives.

As you'll hear, over and over, finding a way to be the best version of ourselves no matter what else is going on is ultimately about awareness. It starts there continues on with being honest with ourselves about where we are succeeding, or struggling. Finally it comes down to embracing the commitment to improve the things that require attention. For example, if your golf swing is more similar to Charles Barkley's, which is less than ideal, but you tell yourself it is akin to Rory McIlroy's, then you're not being very aware or very honest, and thus can't commit to being your best. Similarly, if you're not available to your partner in your relationship, but you tell yourself that you're a regular Casanova, then you can't commit to being the best partner you are capable of being.

With awareness, honesty and commitment in mind, I thought it would be fun to include a self-scoring portion to this book. In each chapter you'll have an opportunity to give yourself a score to par. In golf, par is the number of strokes it should take a scratch (zero handicap) golfer to complete the hole. In this case it's a good way to see where you stand in key areas of your life. This is meant to spark your awareness and sincere self-evaluation so you can decide for yourself what your commitments will be moving forward.

Like everything, the more you put into it, the more you get out of it. And to show that I indeed do not claim to be perfect or to have any of this all figured out, my first self-evaluated score for this book was one over par with 10 pars, 4 birdies, 3 bogeys and 1 double bogey. It's also fun to go back months after your initial score and see if you have improved. I've lowered my score on some significant holes over time. I don't tell you any of this so you can compare yourself to me, but rather so you know that I still have a lot of work to do, too. We are all works in progress. The point is to continue to progress even - and especially - when you don't feel like it. Let's get started.

Scoring Key:

Eagle (-2) – Exceptional. No change needed

Birdie (-1) – Very Good – Room for some improvement

Par (0) – Solid starting point with more work to do

Bogey (+1) – Not good enough. Needs major improvement

Double Bogey (+2) – Critical attention and commitment to improvement needed

Ladies and Gentlemen, next on the tee: Zilosophy on Golf. Enjoy.

Hole 1

Swing Your Swing

"Yep...Inside each and every one of us is one true authentic swing...Somethin' we was born with...Somethin' that's ours and ours alone...Somethin' that can't be taught to ya or learned... Somethin' that got to be remembered...Over time the world can, rob us of that swing...It get buried inside us under all our wouldas and couldas and shouldas.... "
— Bagger Vance (The Legend of Bagger Vance)

I find it completely appropriate to begin this exploration by using a line that was uttered many times by golf's greatest ambassador, Arnold Palmer. "Swing Your Swing." No one understood better than Arnie that as golfers and as people, we are all different, yet we are all on a similar journey. Although our golf swings may fundamentally differ, each of us has the opportunity to maximize our potential. The goal, as Bagger Vance so clearly stated, is for each of us to look inward and find our own truly authentic swing. It's not so much about getting 'better' as it is about digging deep to find the best version of ourselves. It is a version that already exists. All we have to do is locate where it's hiding, which requires peeling away the layers of crap we have placed in the way.

Mr. Palmer had a very unique swing, yet he never tried to change it, or make it more of a 'textbook' swing. On his journey to becoming the most important golfer of all time, Arnold Palmer could have tried to copy Ben Hogan or Sam Snead, who were predecessors and had the type of swing that anyone would want to emulate. Instead, Palmer chose to develop his own golfing style. He recognized that the challenge was to stay true to his unique approach.

In today's context, consider Jim Furyk, whose swing is also unique. How many times have you heard a TV announcer say, "well you wouldn't teach that swing, but it sure works for him?" I would add that it not only works for him, but it IS HIM. Furyk and Palmer both realized that they can't be anyone else. They can only focus on being the best version of who they already are. To try anything else is not only inauthentic, but also detrimental to their game. We all know where Palmer's uniqueness got him, but if you're unfamiliar with Furyk, he has used his distinct swing to become arguably the most consistent golfer in the world for a more than 16-year stretch starting in 2000. He also shot the lowest round ever recorded in PGA Tour competition, posting a remarkable 58 in August of 2016. Both of these examples show how staying true to your authentic self is often critical to success.

I recently heard a story; it was told as part of the coverage of the 2017 US Open at Erin Hills, and was about a golfer in the 1980s. I don't remember his name, not coincidental to the point I am making. The golfer was an up-and-coming star in the game and won a tournament at a very young age. His initial reaction was that he wanted to get even better. He wanted to be, in his words, "perfect." He wanted to have the exact same swing as his mentor, Ben Hogan. What he failed to realize is that no one can have the exact same swing as Ben Hogan, except Ben Hogan. What he didn't understand is that in life, there is no such thing as perfection.

Golf is a constant journey towards being the best version of ourselves that we can possibly be on any given day. It really is that simple, no matter how complicated we are determined to make it. Somewhere along the way I realized that my golf day should not be about the search for perfection, but rather about striving for the absolute best shot possible, one at a time.

The first step in living a life in this way meant learning how to be honest with myself. This was no easy task. I was product of modernity with its constant messaging and advertising telling me that I was not good enough. There's little space for honest reflection in a world that surrounds us with advertising that points out our flaws.

Imagine if we took the black and white interpretation that most seem to have these days about everything to the golf course. I remember a time playing at the K Club in Ireland with my brother-in-law. It was a very windy day, and we both had about 150 yards to get onto the green. He chose to hit a full, high 6-iron so that the wind would grab the ball and throw it right down on the green. I chose to hit a low bump-and-run 8-iron so the ball would stay below the wind and roll up to the green. We both got the ball where it needed to be. Neither was right and neither was wrong. Both were acceptable solutions to the same problem.

Now imagine if we stood there trying to prove that one way was better than the other, as if we were having a political argument. First of all, we would have been there all day freezing our butts off. Secondly, we would have been yet another example of the sad results of competition in our culture. Always the need to be perfect, better than the next guy. It's a shame that we've lost the ability to yield ground to each other and explore alternate views. Finally, we would have literally been arguing about nothing. What's the difference in how we get there, as long as we get there with respect for ourselves and others?

The hidden and incredibly dangerous underlying message is "if you were more like me, then you would be a better golfer" – or on a much grander and more harmful scale - the world would be a better place. Maybe that is true and maybe it isn't. One thing that is certainly true is that we can never be exactly the same. Of course we can learn alternate viewpoints and golf shots from each other. These lessons might lead us to find that best version of our swings or ourselves, and we should all do more of that. But we can't be the same. Our challenge is to find our own swing.

For the record, the world would absolutely not be a better place if we were all the same. Our differences and our uniqueness add color to what would otherwise be a blasé world. Our different views and abilities are the key to a modern inclusive society where we work in concert not in competition. We have to find a way to be more tolerant of varying viewpoints. Play the shot your own way, and take more pleasure in watching the wondrous variety out on the course. We have to redefine our view of perfection as the pursuit of honestly and authentically being the best version of ourselves that we can be, both in the world and on the golf course, on the day that we are currently experiencing.

Let's once again look back at the legacy that Arnold Palmer left behind. He was popular enough that most people know that he was the most influential golfer of all time. Many people may not know that his swing wasn't 'perfect', yet he made it work and became one of the greatest players the game has ever seen. Former pro and golf analyst Peter Jacobson recently said, "Anytime you can be mentioned in the same breath with Arnold Palmer is a very special thing." This is typical of the way he's viewed by peers and fans alike.

There are countless stories about him signing autographs for hours to ensure everyone got their turn, or spending time with sick or underprivileged children, or making sure to look each person he ever met in the eye to truly acknowledge them. My favorite is the story about how Palmer was once leaving a tournament when he noticed a young boy sitting alone. After a brief discussion, he realized the young man was stranded and too shy to admit it. Palmer could've left on his own. Instead, he drove a kid he didn't know all the way home. That kid, named Bobby Clampett, ended up becoming a professional golfer, undoubtedly inspired by that interaction.

Mr. Palmer was not a perfect human being. How can I be so sure? It's simple. To be human is to be flawed. So why then is Arnold Palmer not remembered for his unique swing or his human flaws? It's because every time he stepped on the practice range or the golf course, he was able to summon his very best. He did this out of habit. It was a practice. Every time he stepped out of his house he did the same as a human being. Palmer was honest with himself about his golf game and his approach to life. This is all anyone can ask. With commitment we can also live by this standard.

In a spiritual - or Zilosophical - sense it's not about getting better because we're 'bad' or 'not good enough'. It's about trusting that the best version of us has always been a part of us and then simply choosing that version over the other available options. Sometimes we have to dig deep to find our best way of being, or find our best golf swing. But rest assured, it's always there whenever we want it. We just have to practice the right things in order to coax it out – we'll get into that further on the next hole.

The results of his life tell us that Arnie worked incredibly hard on and off the golf course to give the best he had, as often as he could. Can you say the same? It's time to be honest with yourself and get to work. How good would your golf game and your life be if you were fully committed to this principle?

Score	Explanation	Example
Eagle	You are embracing your uniqueness and working hard to be the best version of yourself.	You started a new charity to save 3-legged alpacas so you could use the wool to clothe refugees.
Birdie	You do well at being your best –but could do more.	You wrote a book because it might help people be better to each other and lower their golf score.
Par	You have average individuality/ self-improvement.	You waited in 4-hour line for the new iPhone, but bought a custom case that no one else has.
Bogey	You follow the crowd because it's easier.	You ordered pizza for dinner again because it's what everyone else wanted.
Double Bogey	You're a sheep with no individuality and no desire to be your best.	You love watching divisive 'news' programs while eating cake and ranting about how stupid 'those other people' are.

Score _____

Pro Tip

One thing that I like to do is to remind myself that I don't have to try to be like anyone else. That is not to say that I am not inspired by the words or actions of others. Rather than emulate or copy them, I try to incorporate the concepts into my own experience. For instance, if I see someone is a good leader, I don't try to lead like them. Instead, I try to use that as inspiration as I develop my own leadership qualities. Another thing I like to do is to remind myself every day that my job is to be the best person I'm capable of being just for that day. Life becomes much more simple by avoiding the pressures of perfectionism and by living in the moment.

Practice Drills

• *Double Bogey* • The first step is becoming aware of your lack of individuality. This week identify 2 to 3 areas in your life where you unconsciously follow the crowd. Write those down and hang them on your mirror or refrigerator.

• *Bogey* • Once you are aware of the areas that need to be addressed come up with a plan for improvement. Instead of ordering pizza again, try 'make your own pizza night' or take the family out to a restaurant with a giant menu so everyone can get what they want without relying on the group to decide. Both of these things promote individuality - especially your own!

• *Par* • It's time to take being your best you to a new level. Interview 2-3 family members or close friends about what they see as your unique qualities. You may or may not agree with the findings, but it's a good idea to find out how others see you. Then pick one thing that you're uniquely good at and really focus on how to use that gift to improve your approach to your job, relationship, or golf game.

Hole 2

Practice Doesn't Make Perfect

"Reverse every natural instinct and do the opposite
of what you are inclined to do, and you will probably
come very close to having a perfect golf swing"
— *Ben Hogan*

Can unchecked habits actually prevent us from reaching a desired goal? Could it have been that the very activities we believed would deliver us a result were actually keeping us from getting what we want? Rather than practicing for the sake of practicing and just going through the motions, we should practice, on and off the course, in a way that will allow us to be our best.

Again being honest is important. Many times we sell ourselves short by saying things like "I don't have the time. I don't have the money - or my personal favorite - I'm just not that good." Any or all of those things might be true. Then again, any or all might be completely false. That's why it is really important to take a hard look and get clear about which barriers are real and which are imaginary. Only then will the best path forward appear.

On hole #1 we explored how your unique golf swing can be a reflection of our unique humanity. We will not contradict that here. Rather, we will explore stripping away perceived barriers that restrict us from finding our true swings and our true selves. What we are talking about is being the best person we are capable of being, and finding the unique golf swing that is ours alone. If our current swing is so awful that it doesn't represent our best effort, then we should search for the one that does.

For almost 20 years, I played the game of golf 'with the swing I was given', which was a horrible slap-fade. I played a lot, went to the range a lot, and because of the repetition I did get more consistent and lowered my scores a bit, but I never really got much better. In fact, I had given up believing that it was possible for me to be much better. Maybe I just wasn't that good of a golfer or an athlete. I was a decent basketball player in high school. I also played some football. I am still one of the best wiffle ball players in America, but that's another book. In any case, my freakish ability on the wiffle ball fields was no help on the golf course. I just didn't have the hand/eye coordination, I thought. I 'didn't have what it takes' to be a good golfer.

Then a very close friend of mine who is a scratch golfer and incredibly gifted hand-eye coordination guy – I mean I won't even play him in ping pong or pool - pleaded with me to let him teach me the fundamentals of a solid swing. After blowing him off for months, I begrudgingly agreed. I remained convinced that there was no hope for me. After just a few quick adjustments and drills, suddenly I was hitting the ball square and making pure contact. I had never felt that before. What the heck had I been doing wrong all those years? All those rounds of golf. All of those hours at the range and then within of a couple of hours I was like a new golfer who could actually play the game. Then it hit me, I had spent all of those countless hours practicing the wrong things and reinforcing bad habits. What a waste!

It's no different off of the golf course. I'm sure many of us have watched our friends repeat the same destructive patterns over and over. We complain about the job we have, or the place we live, or the relationship that we are 'stuck' in. We project this attitude that the universe did this to us. It gave me this crap golf swing, this terrible career or this abusive relationship. I am completely powerless to do anything about it. The truth is that you are powerless to do anything about those things if you keep practicing the same way. This is Einstein's definition of insanity - 'doing the same thing over and over again and expecting different results.'

It is exactly what so many of us do with our lives. We throw our hands up in the air thinking that we're relatively powerless to do anything to make a difference, and then we continue our same destructive behavioral patterns apparently in some twisted attempt to prove that we're right about our own ineptitude. The truth is you can change any situation, but it requires the courage to leave your comfort zone. You can have the career, a relationship, whatever you want, so long as you are willing to be bold enough to jump and rely on patience and faith to know that you'll end up in the right situation.

Back to my story. So I made the swing change, became a scratch golfer and lived happily ever after, right? Nope! This is not a fairy tale and things just don't work like that. It took years to unravel all of my bad habits, and to build the trust and faith that I could get better. It was quite a roller coaster ride. For months I would play great and then for months I felt like I had never hit a golf ball in my life. I remember one particular time, going to play one of my favorite courses, in Oxnard, CA, with my friend/swing coach and a few guys he knew. They knew how good he was but he tried to build me up to show how good a coach he was. He told them how much I'd improved under his tutelage and even went so far as to say that I was a better putter than he is. On this particular day, I was so lost in the transition between swing changes - and exhausted from partying too much that weekend - that I played like complete crap. I sprayed the ball all over the place and consistently hammered putts past the hole while listening to these jerks snicker and make putting comments behind my back. I was furious. But that was just one day and since then I've continued to patiently work and improve. I would bet those judgmental clowns are still pointing out the flaws in others rather than working on their own game.

Even the embarrassment of my swing coach was not my darkest hour. I'll never forget watching a golf tournament and wondering whether I should have just maintained my status quo, and kept my crap swing. I mean was it really worth all of this mental anguish?!? By the way, my original swing was pretty bad. It had a harsh outside/in path, which makes the ball slice hard and takes any chance of power out of the equation. This, combined with a tempo as fast and forced as a kid playing Metallica on the accordion made me appear as if I were suddenly angry at the ground. In fact, 10 year-old once told me that 'if you swing slower, the ball will go further.' The worst thing about hearing this from a little kid is you can't snap at him. You want to say something like, "Thanks, kid. Don't you have a little league game or something? Get out of here. Girls are not the enemy." But you can't. You have to smile and laugh it off.

To make it worse, I knew he was right. Mine was a swing that could inspire laughter among the pros and caddies at the club. A golfing buddy once let me hit an 8 iron in a practice round at the first Tiger-hosted tournament at TPC Boston. The ball landed just off the green and they still cackled at how fundamentally grotesque my swing was. So I did what any self-respecting golfer does in this situation. I went to the clubhouse bar.

Sitting there, drowning my sorrows and moping, I watched the golf tournament on the bar television as Tiger Woods shanked a wedge. It was a complete miss of the most epic proportions. Something we mortals do all the time. And then my brain started racing. Tiger was going through a swing change too, which we would, years later, find out was due to his back pain. He was obviously riding a very similar roller coaster to the one I was on. Well, his was a much more expensive and talented rollercoaster, but the turn of the track looked similar, anyway. By the way, this was the first and only time I have ever been able to relate to Tiger Woods. This guy is a golfing God and switching from one good swing to another. I, on the other hand, have sent countless golf balls into another dimension. I mean total Dr. Who style, just through the trees and gone. But you see, this is exactly the point. If a golfer like Tiger Woods was struggling THAT hard due to a complete swing redesign, well then I was right where I was supposed to be on my path!

In that moment, hope was restored. Actually hope had never gone anywhere. I was just so down on myself and caught up in my head that I couldn't see success any more. As hard as it was to accept, I knew that I had to embrace the challenge before me and realize that sometimes we do indeed need to trudge through some dark days in order to get to the Promised Land. Life is not easy. It's not meant to be. The challenges we are given are meant to make us learn and grow. Golf is not an easy game and it is certainly not meant to be. If we want to learn and grow on and off the course we must make an honest and unbiased assessment of our 'game' and then commit fully to the right kind of practice.

Just to wrap up my story - as it stands today - I am currently a 13 handicap, which is far better than the 22+ I produced back then. I have also broken 80 a handful of times, which would have never been possible with my old swing. I recently made my first hole in one, which would only have been possible by dumb luck with my previous swing.

I continue to work on my game, not in the pursuit of perfection. These days I'm more interested in reaching my full potential. Like everyone else, some days (and rounds) are better than others, but I've learned something from each experience.

Tomorrow morning, take a step back and assess whether you are practicing the things that will deliver the results that you want. It's too easy to run on autopilot and assume that everything is "fine," because things are the way they've always been. Maintaining the status quo is comfortable, but it might be holding you back from being your best.

Is comfort really more important than fulfilling your true potential? Are you practicing things in life and golf that will make you better? Are you mired in your old way of doing things just because it's all you know?

Score	Explanation	Example
Eagle	You're always practicing things that make you better.	You learned to play the piano at the age of 70 to keep your brain sharp and spend time with your grandson.
Birdie	You're sometimes practicing the right things.	You joined a book club to force you to read more.
Par	You get stuck between old habits and new possibilities.	You went for a run and then ate a pint of ice cream.
Bogey	You are stuck in old habits that don't serve you.	You binge watched entire series of Law and Order, for the 3rd time.
Double Bogey	You're a curmudgeon who is comfortable the 'way you are' even though it's not good.	You were bored so you got drunk and spent the rent money at the casino.

Score _____

Pro Tip

Ask for help. Whether you're trying to improve something in your golf game or in another area of your life, the best thing you can do is seek advice/coaching from someone who actually knows something about the area in which you are hoping to improve. And it should be someone who is not trying to change who you are at your fundamental core, but rather someone who is willing and able to work with your unique abilities and coax out your full potential. Having coaching also makes me feel accountable for best efforts as opposed to working on things in a vacuum where it's easy to give up.

Practice Drills

◆ Double Bogey ◆ If you have bad habits with serious consequences, it's a good idea to talk to someone about them. Saying it out loud will force you to admit there's a problem. Identify one or two areas that need critical attention and talk to a friend, a coach, or a therapist. There is no shame in seeking help. It's very common and you'll be glad that you reached out.

◆ Bogey ◆ Get a coach. Whether it's something in your personal life or in your golf game, engage with someone who can create a program that will allow you to practice in a way that addresses weaknesses and builds upon strengths.

◆ Par ◆ Write down your goals for the day, week, month and year. Come up with a plan and stick to the practice routine that will work for you. Once you've identified what needs to be done, the commitment to the regimen becomes paramount.

Hole 3

Confidence Is Key

"Confidence is the most important single factor in this game, and no matter how great your natural talent, there is only one way to obtain and sustain it: work."
— Jack Nicklaus

Confidence is such a key component to playing good golf. It's simply impossible to play well without it. As Mr. Nicklaus points out, there is no easy path to confidence. It doesn't just appear out of thin air. We just talked about practicing the things that give us the greatest chance to uncover our highest capabilities. Now it's time to practice those things so much that we don't have to think about them anymore. They just happen, because we know we've put in the required effort.

Jack was referring to golf but he could just as easily have been referring to life itself. Confidence not only fueled his game to the point where it made him the greatest champion of all time. He won 18 major championships and came in second 19 times. But it clearly drove his family life and business career as well. You don't design over 300 golf courses worldwide without having incredible belief in your abilities.

True confidence isn't bred overnight. It takes practice and repetition until it becomes part of you. You don't even have to think about it. You know that you can do it so there is nothing to think about; you *Just Do It.* This is why professional golfers spend as much as 8-10 hours practicing per day.

It's no accident that Tiger Woods dominated golf for the period of time that he did. Yes, he had incredible natural ability, and then he just worked harder than anybody else. In fact, he was maniacal about practice and training. In the early 2000s, his DAILY training routine consisted of the following: running four miles, lifting weights, hitting balls for 2-3 hours on the range, playing a full round of golf, working on short game for a couple hours, running another 4 miles and finally playing basketball or tennis. Most people couldn't do all that in a week! It's no wonder that he had completely unmatched confidence every time he stepped on the golf course. He was in better physical and mental shape and had hit more golf balls than anyone else in the field.

Sustaining confidence is challenging. This leads us to another of Nicklaus' famous statements about golf. "It takes hundreds of good shots to gain confidence but only one bad one to lose it." We must spend hours and hours of repetition on any task that we want to approach with an assuredness that will deliver success. Yet one tiny little slip-up can send us spinning out of control, and suddenly our insecurities will snowball at an alarming rate. When this happens – and it happens to all of us – it's incredibly difficult to slow or stop the decent.

In the summer of 2010, my girlfriend got me onto Riviera Country Club for my birthday. I was to play with two of my best friends and a member that was hosting us. I was so excited to play this iconic course that had hosted the LA Open since the 1920s. I had studied the history and I wanted to go see Bogey's tree at the 12th hole, where Humphrey Bogart would sit and drink Jack Daniels while watching the tournament just below Audrey Hepburn's house. Then there was the par three 6th hole, which uniquely contains a bunker in the middle of the green. I had watched tournaments played on the course on TV since I was a kid.

What had me almost as excited was that I had just started to feel comfortable with the change I'd incorporated into my swing. I actually had a chance to play well! I had a great warm up session on the driving range and was striking the ball perfectly. We got to the raised tee at the par 5 first hole and I hit a decent tee shot and I made par on that hole. It would be my last par of the day. On the 2nd hole I hit a bad shot and all of that confidence I had going into the round disappeared like Bogey walking into the mist.

Suddenly I was left with nothing but fear and the memory of my bad swing. It really happened that fast and I never recovered. I still was able to hit some great shots that day, like the 50-yard bunker shot I hit to two feet from the hole, but they were few and far between. After that round I had a lot of collateral damage to clean up in order to restore my confidence. It was like the golfing version of PTSD. I had to get back to work and once again put in the required hours and repetition to build my confidence back up.

I will talk more about the dangers of self-criticism later in the book. For now, we're just exploring how fragile and fleeting confidence can be. The trick is to remember that we can choose our best swing or our worst swing. We can choose our best version of ourselves, or our worst version. But at the end of the day, confidence is a choice. The more we work and practice the more comfortable we become in the moments when we must choose that confident swing or that confident self.

There are two sides to the golf game. The physical side and the mental side. In 2017, I was working with a young player, who had just turned pro, on the mental side of his game. He was a talented player with a lot of potential. He had a great swing but as with most people in their early 20s, he needed some guidance in other key areas. When we sat to talk about his daily routine, I was stunned to find out that he wasn't hitting at least 500 putts a day. Not only that, he had never even hit 500 putts in one session before! I explained to him that he would be handcuffing himself against the field when most or all of the other competitors were hitting thousands upon thousands of practice putts per week, not merely because of the muscle memory involved, but much more importantly, but because of the confidence that comes from knowing that you've put the necessary time in.

"Drive for show. Putt for dough." This is one of the most popular sayings in the game of golf, because the final stroke that gets the ball into the hole is generally the most important one. This is why many instructors start teaching golf in reverse from the green to the tee. As a professional, one has to believe she is the best putter in the field in order to win tournaments. That is the amount of confidence required to compete at that level. Just look at streaky putters like Adam Scott and Sergio Garcia. They are two of the best ball strikers in the world but it still comes down to the 'flat stick'. When they putt well they win. When they don't putt well, even players of their caliber struggle to win. It then stands to reason, if one wants to compete professionally, then one must invest countless hours of putting practice in order to build supreme confidence.

This same concept should be applied to other areas of our lives where we want to build confidence. It takes serious commitment and hours upon hours of repetition to figure out how to do a thing so well that it becomes second nature. It doesn't matter if we want to be a more confident golfer; or have more confidence in dating; or to be a confident performer on stage. It takes hours and hours of practicing the right things in the right way.

How would you score your confidence on and off of the golf course? Is there more work you could be doing to achieve the poise you would like to attain?

Score	Explanation	Example
Eagle	You have the quiet confidence of a lion in the jungle.	You wanted to sing a song for your husband's 50th birthday so you took lessons and practiced for 2 years.
Birdie	You are pretty confident but have more work to do.	You knew the speech inside and out so you didn't review the notes the night before and got a B plus instead of an A minus.
Par	You get a glimpse of confidence and then it evaporates.	You finally got that girl's number at the bar but didn't call because you 'didn't know what to say'.
Bogey	Confidence remains elusive.	You only go to parties with a group of friends and only talk to them once there.
Double Bogey	You give yourself a vote of no confidence.	You always sit in the back of class next to the door so you can be the first one to leave and not have to talk to anyone.

Score _____

Pro Tip

Repetition is the key to building confidence. Once you have identified things to practice, which will help you get better, then you have to be relentless about practicing those things. This means you have to build a schedule that will allow the necessary hours to gain self-belief. Take some time to think about how you could rearrange your schedule to practice more.

Practice Drills

◆ *Double Bogey* ◆ Start small and use golf as a way to teach you how practice can build confidence. Commit to practicing putting at home in your hallway or living room for 10 minutes a day. Do this every day for a month and see how much more confident you are with your putter the next time you play.

◆ *Bogey* ◆ Challenge yourself to do something that seems terrifying to you. If you don't feel comfortable meeting strangers, sign up for a speed-dating event. The goal isn't necessarily to get a date, but to practice talking to people under difficult circumstances so it will seem much easier the next time there are less stressful conditions. Who knows? You might get a date, too!

◆ *Par* ◆ Take music lessons of an instrument that you've never played. This will force you to practice something that you are not good at. It will also show you, after hours and hours of repetition, how good you eventually get. This is the routine of building confidence through work.

Hole 4

Mind Games

"You swing your best when you have the fewest things to think about"
— Bobby Jones

We've allowed - if not willed - our world to become an incredibly chaotic place with constant connection and commotion. Our minds are filled with clutter and we are constantly racing as we try to keep up with the unsustainable pace of work, social and family lives. Some people have surmised that we are now more like 'human doings' than human beings. Many times it's all we can do to survive the daily grind, all so we can pass out, only to get up and do it all over again the next day. Suddenly a whole month, year, decade or entire lifetime has gone by and we never took the time to rest our minds and be present to moments as they occur. If that sounds like a dark view, it is. And we all do it all the time.

The real tragedy here is that we think that we have to be thinking, processing, analyzing all the time in order to be successful or relevant. This couldn't be further from the truth. As powerful and amazing as our human brains are they can also be a hindrance. Think about having to maintain the kind of frenetic pace of life that I just described and what that does to your mind. Now imagine that you suddenly have a 4-hour window to escape and play golf. Good luck playing well, pal. How in the world can anyone play good golf with all that crap running around in your head?

As Sam Snead put it, "Thinking instead of acting is the number one golf disease." Okay, Sam, so then tell me how I'm supposed to stay grounded and focused when my mind is constantly racing? I'm like Ray Liota at the end of Goodfellas with the sauce and the helicopter keeps following me. And my manager said something a little mysterious on Friday, and my kid got into trouble at school. But Sam wants me to clear my mind. What is this, *Kung Fu*? Now add to this the fact that there are many things about which I might actually want to think about: keep your head down; keep your body still; swing around your body; smooth tempo; keep the club face square; aim at the target; make solid contact; follow through, etc. etc. So I've got Sam Snead and the Buddhist monks on one shoulder telling me to be only in the present. I've got the updates from the twenty applications on my mobile phone telling me everything that changes in the world the moment it happens. I've got the collected wisdom of golfing coaches on the other shoulder providing directions on exactly how to move every part of my body. Is it any surprise that some golfers end up looking like the stiff guy playing Twister? It's almost impossible to make a good swing on the ball when the last thing on your mind is... the ball. At some point we have to key on one or two 'swing thoughts' and just hit the darn ball! A swing thought is a simple idea, a languid phrase, a placid image that keeps your mind occupied just enough to box out the rest of life.

I've recently started to put my cell phone in my golf bag when I play. I do this only when it seems possible, and the events in my life don't seem as pressing. Sometimes I like to keep score with an app on my phone, so on those occasions I'll keep it out. However, when I do this, I usually end up getting sucked into checking email, browsing social media, checking sports scores or the weather forecast. This is my life. I'm so connected that I've lost connection with the game I'm trying to play. Instead of taking in the scenery, and connecting with playing companions, focusing on the task at hand, I end up daydreaming rather than being fully present and in the moment. In fact, as I'm typing this I've checked 3 emails and 2 texts. I'm not proud of this, but at least I'm being honest. Golf can be the path that leads us to greater focus. In order to do that, we first have to start with the basics by learning ways to remove the clutter.

I don't know about you, but I am much more effective in every aspect of my life when I feel free from the constant barrage of thoughts and anxieties that modern life can produce. I'm better when I'm well rested. And I've found that meditation is a great way to slow my mind down and focus. Now I'm not saying you need to move into an Ashram and learn how to clap with one hand. A person can meditate in a parked car. Athletes often talk about the 'flow state,' while running, cycling, shooting hoops. Artists also talk about the feeling of losing yourself in an activity. So whether it's a jigsaw puzzle, the putting green, or knitting, I'm saying embrace that feeling and allow yourself to disengage from the world.

A formal practice of meditation can have a powerful and positive impact on a person's life. Guided meditation allows a person to develop a specific mental skill; the ability to let go of the world and focus on *being* rather than *doing*. This is how you get real rest for your brain. A Harvard University study recently proved that not only does regular meditation lead to reduced anxiety, better sleep, better brain function and all of the other benefits we've just described, but after 8 weeks it can even help regenerate the grey matter in your brain. By learning to quiet the mind, the brain can actually heal itself! (There's hope for me yet.) And while most golfers aren't seeking to heal their brains, there remains a near universal search for clarity-of-mind and waking rest. Why can't we bring these two worlds together? The philosophical traditions of the Far East and the needs of the golfer are the two friends you know who should be dating.

American Tibetan Buddhist, Pema Chodron, talks about the benefits and dangers of a mind unchecked. She states, "The mind is the source of all suffering, and it is also the source of all happiness. When something comes up in your life that causes you dissatisfaction, or triggers habitual patterns and reactivity, or makes you angry, lonely, and jealous, ask yourself: Are these emotions happening because of outer circumstances? Are they completely dependent on outer circumstances? The path of meditation says that we have to work with our mind, and that if we do work with our mind, the outer circumstances become workable."

OK, this is all great, but what does it have to do with golf? EVERYTHING!!! How many incredibly talented golfers have we lost in the forests of distraction? How many talented young men and women could've enjoyed an elite professional career, if not for the sand traps of untethered synapses? Think about that the next time you're playing golf. No wait don't think about that. I'm just kidding.

We can have all the talent in the world and still not be very good under pressure, and if we struggle in these moments, it's probably because we can't seem to get our mind right. This is why some of the top golfers work with sports psychologists. Sports psychologists help athletes train their minds to have positive thoughts during competition. This undoubtedly helps but to me it misses a key point. What we need to do is to train the mind to shut the heck up and get out of the way, and this comes from meditative practice. Not coincidentally as golf has grown in popularity, we have seen a rise in the number of players who feel comfortable practicing formal meditation as an important element of their training regimen.

I remember playing at Malibu Country Club in the summer of 2000. I was about to get married a couple days later, so I scheduled a round of golf with friends and family that were in town. Anyone who has planned a wedding and experienced the logistical challenges associated with the joining of two families knows how much anxiety and stress can build as the event approaches. And that doesn't even include the emotional thoughts that seem to relentlessly batter the brain. So there I was one beautiful day in Malibu, surrounded by friends and laughing a lot. Yet I have no clear recollection of the round I played, or any of the shots that I hit, which should be of no surprise, as I was there physically but not mentally. Although I do have a faint memory that I believe I swung and missed the ball entirely on the first tee. Turns out it's difficult to make pure contact, or in this case any contact, when your mind is elsewhere.

What I learned that day in Malibu was that no matter what is happening around us, there are two important things that must happen on the golf course. First, we must allow our intuition - our gut instinct - to have a more powerful voice. Sometimes it's better to allow that voice to choose our next shot. It will guide us as we find the best way through the course, but only if your intuition is calm and steady. If our minds are busy, and if we are changing our minds every 3 seconds, then it may be time to ignore this voice. Secondly, finding inner quiet allows a golfer to begin again with a clean slate, to rebuild and stretch the canvas upon which we will paint our masterpiece. Let intuition be an aid and not a hindrance. No matter what situation we encounter in life, whether playing in a weekly Saturday match or meeting with coworkers on a dreary Friday afternoon, the more we can learn to just be with it as it is, the more things will start to simply fall effortlessly into place, and into our favor. It's time to scream 'Stop the ride. I wanna get off!' and allow our brains a break.

How are you fairing with regard to taking the time to turn your brain off and let it rest? Are you constantly plugged in and being held hostage by unyielding thoughts swimming in your head?

Score	Explanation	Example
Eagle	You are a master at shutting off your mind and listening to your intuition.	You meditate 3 hours every morning like the Dalai Lama.
Birdie	You are an expert at keeping thoughts in check.	You go for a bike ride every morning to clear your mind and start each day fresh.
Par	You're usually pretty Zen but thoughts still creep in at inopportune times.	You are typically thinking about your grocery list while at yoga class.
Bogey	You have difficulty turning off your thoughts.	You sleep with the TV on all night. Every night.
Double Bogey	Your brain is always buzzing 24/7.	You listen to an audio book to study for a test while writing that report for work with the football game on the TV.

Score _____

Pro Tip

Find a way to incorporate some sort of meditation into your life. Traditional meditation is the most tried-and-true type of practice that will help. There are many books and apps that can help you find a practice that works for you. Then again, if you can achieve this by going for a run, walk, paddleboard ride, yoga class, by all means do what works. Any activity that helps you turn your mind off and 'zone out' is what we are looking for here. A clear mind is an imperative starting point for manifesting your desires in life and golf, so start there.

Practice Drills

✦ *Double Bogey* ✦ Find a time to take a break in the middle of your day to step away from your desk, schoolwork or home duties and rather than stare at your phone or TV to decompress for 15 minutes, try turning everything off, closing your eyes and just listening to your breath. Don't judge your thoughts. Let them come and go. Just focus on your breath.

✦ *Bogey* ✦ Download a meditation app. I use *Insight Timer* but find one you like. Then for a week try a guided meditation for 10 minutes at the beginning and end of your day every day.

✦ *Par* ✦ Before your next round of golf find a quiet place and to take 5 minutes and close your eyes and get grounded. Then commit to leaving your phone in your car or turning it off and leaving it in your golf bag for the entire round. Be sure to warn your wife or boyfriend before doing this.

Hole 5

Re:Vision

"Put your eyes on Bobby Jones...Look at his practice swing, almost like he's searchin' for something...Then he finds it... Watch how he settle hisself right into the middle of it, feel that focus...He got a lot of shots he could choose from...Duffs and tops and skulls, there's only ONE shot that's in perfect harmony with the field...One shot that's his, authentic shot, and that shot is gonna choose him...There's a perfect shot out there tryin' to find each and every one of us...All we got to do is get ourselves out of its way, to let it choose us...."
— Bagger Vance, (The Legend of Bagger Vance)

Now that we've learned to calm our mind, what do we do with all that quiet space? That's the beauty of it. We can now choose how to fill that space with anything. So why not choose positive images? Thoughts about how we want the world and our life to be? Why not thoughts of a better golf game? Often we don't realize that we are constantly visualizing and manifesting our reality already. It's just that our heads our so packed full of crap that we are subconsciously visualizing chaos and disappointment. With a blank - or at least uncluttered - canvas we are free to consciously choose the positive images that we want to manifest into our desired reality.

In recent years there are a couple of great examples of elite golfers that have done this on the golf course at a high level. Jason Day and JB Holmes do exactly what Bagger Vance described in that movie scene about Bobby Jones. Watching Day or Holmes when they are at their best, you can practically see them quieting their own mind and searching for the right swing. You can almost hear their inner monologue, as they search for a particular shot and then, in a moment, they seem to be in a trance-like state. It's subtle and it only lasts for a few brief seconds, but in that space they visualize the perfect shot. The shot that will solve the riddle of the hole. You can see the moment of realization unfurl across a great golfer's face. In the moment that they actually see the shot. It's almost as if the shot has already happened, and what we are watching is just the eventual physical result, a byproduct of deep concentration. The sound of crickets humming, a distant airplane slowly ripping the page of the sky, and a single golfer reaching deep into the universe to extract the required shot.

When I say that you can see them go through the visualization process I do mean it literally. Watch the footage from JB Holmes' win at the Shell Houston Open in 2015. He actually closes his eyes for a few seconds before every shot. Obviously, he played great in all facets of his game to win, but visualization was definitely a key component. I have always found it curious that a few months after that tournament he seemed to be less and less committed to that regimen. Despite playing at a very high level and being in contention a lot, he hasn't won since (as of publishing time). I can't help but wonder if that one little practice might be the difference to put him over the edge for his next win. Easy for me to say. He's a great golfer and I'm sure it will happen soon for him.

From that same year, a golf fan can also watch any of Jason Day's five wins. During this period, he climbed the golf rankings and set the golf world ablaze while capturing his first major. I was amazed watching his pre-shot routine. You could see him settle himself down, and into what could have only been a quieting-the-mind routine. His eyes would close half way, almost to the point where he looked like he'd been possessed. This seemed like more than just visualizing success, it was physical and intense. It seemed to change the mood of the area around him. You could almost feel and see his next shot. Unlike Holmes, Day has remained regimented in this process, and you can probably still see him doing this today.

There is a lot that goes into winning on the PGA Tour. You need every edge you can get. Jack Nicklaus said that he never hit a shot - not even in practice – without first seeing a sharp picture of it in his mind. Many will remember Jack's amazing victory at the '86 Masters, where he won at the age of 46. Apparently the night before the final round, with an outside chance to win if he played really well, he was getting treatment by a trainer. As he was being worked on, he visualized how he needed to play each and every hole the next day. He saw the clubs that he would choose, the flight of the ball, the location after the tee shot, and curve of each putt along the sloping greens. The round went eerily similar to the way he had envisioned it. He won his 6th and final Masters this way. He committed to the practice of visualization. Imagining the first shot and each one after is an edge that you want to have in any endeavor. I have used this technique to yield much more modest positive results in my golf game.

Quantum physics has recently proven that everything we can see, touch, and feel is made of 99.9999% energy. Maybe this has something to do with manifesting visualizations, because mental pictures are energy, too. Look, I'm not trying to tell you that I can prove string theory. All I'm saying is that when I allow myself to connect to the energy, and when I am able to remove any thoughts that block this connection, I have a better chance of making what I visualize a reality. The phrase we sometimes hear is, 'manifest your dreams.' It can sound a little like a visit to the palm reader, but there is truth in this phrase. And golfers like us prove it every weekend when we imagine something we shouldn't be able to do, and then it happens.

I was once playing in a charity golf tournament in Long Beach, CA with some good friends. Not the good friends from Malibu. Different group, but just as funny. It was a course we had all played many times, and quite frankly, it was one I'd never played all that well. Anyway, It was another day at Lakewood CC and I was hitting it all over the place. I clobbered a worm burner down the third fairway. Then I nearly took out a bird on the 7th tee. By the time we got to the 13th tee, I was search for a disguise in my golf bag. And it didn't help that this hole was a monster. I mean a 210-yard Kraken of a par 3, that required a long shot over the water, and then a soft touch uphill if you want to stop the ball at the top and near the flagstick. As it was a charity tournament there was a pretty young girl watching from the tee box, because a hole-in-one would win you a new car. Wait a minute, I don't know why the pretty girl was there. Maybe the car company had sent her. Anyway she had long brown hair, and swimming pool blue eyes. I don't remember what kind of car it was.

As we were waiting for the green to clear, my friends and I were joking around and teasing each other about how pretty this girl was. To be clear, it was all very respectful, like a bunch of school kids anxiously giggling at a cute classmate. Anyhow, the hole was playing 220 yards that day and I had the perfect club – my Callaway 2-hybrid. I looked my buddy right in the eye and said this one is for Jenny (or whatever her name was). As I teed the ball up, I told myself that I had to impress this girl and that's all I was thinking about. Not the angle of my swing, or the phone messages I hadn't checked, not the width of my stance or the falling prices on the NASDAQ. My best swing was there in the recesses of my mind, and summoned by the image of that siren in the distance, I reared back and let the golf gods guide my fate. My best swing is exactly what I delivered on that day. If you've been golfing long enough, you probably have a memory like this as well. It's the memory that jumps to the front of your mind when someone uses that phrase, 'the best ball you ever hit.' I struck the ball with a purity that is elusive. I ripped one right at the flag, and it came within inches of winning that car. Walking off the tee box, I winked at Jenny and drove off. Mission accomplished.

Similarly, as we can imagine our next golf shot like we want it to be, we can also imagine all the things that we want in life like we want them to be. But let's be clear, visualization is not a genie in a bottle. We can't just wish for things and call it a visualization. Manifesting your visualizations takes practice. Start small and work at it. Don't visualize a Dustin Johnson tee shot if you've never hit one farther than 150 yards. Aim for more than you've done before and see it fly down the middle.

Years ago, every time I would stand over the ball to putt, I would imagine Steve Stricker's putting stroke - pure relaxation in his shoulders, soft hands, smooth pendulum tempo, pure contact. I haven't yet and probably won't ever turn into the putter that Stricker is, but I can tell you without a shred of doubt that the practice of imagining him while putting for a few years made me a MUCH better putter.

We can all visualize but we must learn what works for each of us in terms of visualization. I was once working with a young golfer and after a few holes, he turned to me and said, "I don't know how to visualize." I was ready for this one. I said "of course you do. Have you ever imagined anything in your mind as a kid or as an adult? That's visualization." Some people will clearly see the shot. Some people will just have a feeling about the shot. Some might even imagine the sound of perfect contact between the club and the ball. Find what works for you and do that.

Seve Ballesteros was one of golf's greatest champions from the late 70's to the mid-90's. He seemed to come out of nowhere to finish second in the 1978 Open Championship as a 19 year-old. But if you know his story, you know that he didn't just suddenly become one of the greatest golfer's in the world. No one worked harder or dreamed more about being a great golfer than Seve. As a young boy growing up in a small, coastal fishing village in Spain, he would spend hours daydreaming about being a golfer. He also spent hours practicing with makeshift clubs that he patched together with sticks. All of those thousands of shots he hit over the Spanish countryside. The many hours practicing on the beaches went into his mental database of shots. This was what he could call forth many years later. So much practice had bred familiarity with a great variety of swings. The muscle memory and the likely action of the ball off of the club face. The angle of trajectory relative to wind conditions. It was a deep reservoir of visualizations that could adapt to the present day situation, and the shot he needed. This is how he became the best shot-maker the game has ever seen.

Yet all those hours of practice weren't solely responsible for Ballesteros becoming the best golfer in the world in the mid-80's. He said, "In my mind, I always dreamt and believed I was a champion." This is not a small statement. He literally spent thousands of hours visualizing himself as being THE BEST golfer. We've forgotten what it's like to be a child and dream about what we want in life. Somewhere along the way we started thinking that daydreams don't come true. But the truth is they do if you stay committed and do not lose faith that eventually they will become a reality.

Seve's story also teaches us that using visualization to become a better golfer does not have to be limited to the golf course. Imagining a swing and seeing the shots we'll hit before we get to the course will also make us better. This comes in really handy for those who live in cold climates and can't hit the range during winter months.

I'm not saying that visualization is magic pixie dust. I'm saying that we can use visualization to our advantage by mentally practicing while we're at home, or while doing a trivial activity that doesn't require much mental focus. We can similarly take 5 to 10 minutes out of the day to imagine that new job, new car, or new relationship is going to happen. The mere act of imagination will in fact bring you closer to what you desire. We are already visualizing whether we are aware of it or not. The trick is to remain conscious so that you can proactively visualize the things you want instead of reactively visualizing the things you fear.

Are you consciously using the power of visualization to your advantage both on and off of the golf course? Or are you letting fear control your subconscious and wreak havoc in your life?

Score	Explanation	Example
Eagle	Your visualizations help you manifest the things you want in life.	Like Jim Carey you wrote yourself a $10 million check with nothing in the bank and it turned into real money.
Birdie	You have 20/20 visualization.	You used Jedi mind tricks and visualization to get that promotion at work.
Par	Sometimes you consciously visualize, and others you do not.	Nailed your board presentation at work but can't figure out why your kids are a nightmare.
Bogey	Can't seem to manifest the things you want.	Fear caused you to miss five 3-foot putts in your Saturday match and you lost the money to buy that new driver you've been drooling over.
Double Bogey	You subconsciously call chaos into your life.	You got fired and dumped in the same day then got into a car accident on the way home and wonder, "why does this keep happening"?

Score _____

Pro Tip

This tip is connected to the previous one, as you can't visualize what you really want if you haven't cleared all the crap out of your head first. So, the best time to visualize is just after –or during – your meditative practice. In fact, there are some great, guided meditations out there that are specific to golf and sports in general. I have had incredible success with this on and off of the golf course. I will often visualize every hole and how I want to play them prior to playing. Years before I started writing this book, I would regularly visualize my life to include travel, lots of golf, speaking engagements and book signings. Now it's all happening!

Practice Drills

• *Double Bogey* • Now pick one thing you would like to manifest in your golf game and one thing you would like to manifest that has nothing to do with golf. Then spend five minutes a day visualizing those things – ideally during meditation at first.

• *Bogey* • Be the Martin Scorsese of your own biopic. Visualize how you would make a film about how your life will unfold beginning now. Close your eyes for twenty minutes and imagine how you want your life to be. Think of the car you want to drive, the job you would love or the relationship you've always wanted. Practice this regularly and you'll be surprised (maybe even a little freaked out) by how much power you have to manifest your desires.

• *Par* • The next time you are going to play a golf course that you have previously played, spend 20 minutes the night before, the morning of, or both, visualizing every single shot you want to play on every single hole. Spend some time beforehand refreshing your memory of the course map.

Hole 6

The Moment
Of Impact

*"The point is that it doesn't matter if you look like
a beast before or after the hit, as long as you look like
a beauty at the moment of impact"*
— Seve Ballesteros

As 'human doings', we've made it really hard on ourselves to be present and to live in the moment. The vast majority of us do not live our lives or play our games in 'the now,' and we pay a hefty price for lack of focus. I have struggled with this. I know what it means to allow my fears of the past and the future to shape my present moment, making me unable to fully experience the moment that I'm in. Beating ourselves up for struggling with this only continues the cycle of worry. This is the sad reality in which many of us exist...and in which most of us play golf.

As Eckhart Tolle profoundly points out in *The Power of Now*, "The past gives you an identity and the future holds the promise of salvation, of fulfillment in whatever form. Both are illusions.... Nothing has happened in the past; it happened in the Now. Nothing will ever happen in the future; it will happen in the Now...Realize deeply that the present moment is all you have. Make the NOW the primary focus of your life."

How I work to stay in the now: I visualize the shot, commit to moment of impact and, then let go of any attachment to the outcome.

The idea of merging these concepts came to me quite literally in a dream. I realize that sounds a little weird, but I think is the good kind of weird, and as a great friend of mine likes to remind me, "The truth is often stranger than fiction." It was only a couple of days after first experiencing this dream that I found myself on a golf course off the 210 freeway, outside of Los Angeles. My friends and I had never played there before, and it was a brisk fall day. I was wearing gloves and I thought, "OK today I'm just going to focus on this concept and nothing else. Visualize. Commit to impact. Release attachment to outcome. No other swing thoughts." I had passively used visualization and releasing attachment to outcome on the golf course, but I had never committed to doing this on every shot.

Standing on the tee of 3rd hole, a short 125-yard par 3 that faded slightly uphill, I drew a pitching wedge from my bag. It was the perfect club given my calculations. With calm and focus I went through the process as I had outlined. I made my swing, I felt that feeling – and heard that sound – when you make perfect contact. The ball was off and it was out of my hands. I was present. In the now. It never left the flagstick and as it approached the green, and it looked like it might go in. My knees buckled a little at the thought of what might happen and then it went right over top of the flagstick and stopped 2 feet from the hole. I had just missed my first hole in one. And this was not because of luck. It was a feeling we all know when something happens as a result of skill and focus. It was there beside the distant hum of a California freeway that I had a deeply profound thought: *holy crap this totally works*!

Presence is a must if you want to play well and enjoy our next round of golf. When my mind drifts back and forth between the past and the future, like the ebbs and flows of a tide on the beach, I cannot be fully committed to the most important 70-100 now moments that occur during a golf game. These are my collected moments of impact. When I stop and think about it, this is what golf is to me. This is the essence of the game; a series of now moments of impact that will eventually add up to a final score. This is what made Tiger Woods, at his peak, one of the greatest golfers we've ever seen. No matter how badly he had hit the previous shot, he was always able to summon the mental toughness to let the immediate past go. He could then completely commit himself to the next shot. He almost never seemed to let a prior miss bleed over into his current shot. He had the will to stay in the exact moment as it was happening.

Leading up to our trip to play Old Head Golf Links in Kinsale, Ireland, my friend called me almost every day to talk about the 12th hole. Look it up if you've never seen it. It could be the most beautiful hole in golf. A towering cliff runs along the entire left side of the hole, which crawls alongside the Celtic sea. My friend was beyond obsessed with the opportunity to play this gem. I'm not exaggerating; he talked about it every day for months. Walking up the 11th fairway, he looked at me and said, "you know what hole is next right?" I chuckled and said, "Maybe we should finish this hole first."

After a few more swings, we were finally at the tee box on glorious number 12 at Old Head. Months of anticipation had built up to this moment. You can probably guess what happened next. My friend proceeded to top his tee shot, which rolled 10 yards and leapt off the cliff. I have the video to prove it. He thought about that shot for months. When the moment finally came, fear of the bad swings he'd taken in the past reared up and took over. His past would not allow him to stay in the moment of impact. What was to be his glorious moment was ruined (insert the sound of a very small violin playing).

In my everyday life, I've discovered the same thing can be true. Maybe you've had a similar experience. You suddenly arrive at the end of a series of life events, an exchange that comes at the end of a chain of moments of impact. And you sense a certain perspective, as if the present scene is the cumulative result of so many previous deeds. The more present we are to those calculations, the more fulfilling lives we will lead and the better our golf scores will be.

Fear has no place in a well-played round of golf, or in a life that is lived in the present. All the fears that I have dragged from my past, or projected into my future, have only served to keep me distracted from the moments that I might otherwise enjoy or control. Know the feeling? The sense that a part of our lives have been in some way compromised, and instead of composing our own symphony of dreams and desires, we've instead felt stuck, mired in a version of life that has us complaining to ourselves (however quietly) about the way things happened or the way they should be. If we are aware of these feelings than we are remembering the moments when we let the errant shots of the past dictate our swing in the present. I'm no expert, but I will tell you that I believe trust is the key. We must trust our swing on the course - believe that we can execute the swing that we imagine - and know that our desired outcomes beyond the course are possible.

Earlier I talked about how important it is to clear your mind in order to make space for positive visualizations on and off the course. Now it's time to fully commit to the moment of impact with a presence of mind, body and soul. In the context of a golf swing, it's all right to say that we will quiet our thoughts and see the perfect shot. We will focus towards making pure contact in that split second where the club hits the ball. We will believe that it will happen and we will focus that belief squarely into that brief moment of impact.

Here's the really cool part. Once we've made contact, we are on to a new moment. The follow through is natural and the moment of impact is gone. It can no longer be controlled. The outcome is written and we can only watch until the ball comes to rest. We've done our part and now we must release attachment to outcome. What do the golf gods have in store for us? Maybe we get an attempt at a 6-foot birdie putt. Maybe we get the opportunity to get up and down from the bunker. It does not matter. It is out of our hands and we get to be present and watch with wonder as it unfolds before our eyes. As my good friend and PGA tour winner Jason Gore once told me, "Hit the ball. Find it. Hit it again." Elegant and simple advice from a master of the game.

When we are at home, at the office, or in another social setting, the same rules apply. Clear the mind. Visualize the result. Let go of attachment. Commit to the moment and be present. This is how we make a life. The outcome is often as wondrous and elusive as the landing spot of the ball. All we can do is do the best we can, in this moment, and in this moment, and in this moment, and on and on and on. By staying completely connected to each and every moment that we are gifted we actually do get to create life as we want it to be.

The choice is ours. We can allow our regrets or our anxieties to frame our reality or we can take responsibility for the shots we take during our round of golf. The time is now. And that needs to be our focus. Now is the only thing that is ever happening. Any other thoughts just serve to pull your awareness elsewhere.

By the way, I almost forgot to mention that none of this is easy. Life and golf are not easy and they are not meant to be. If they were, we'd all be very bored. It takes incredible commitment and determination to learn how to be present at all times. I certainly haven't achieved nirvana in that sense, but as I continue to stay with it, I become more and more present and in control.

How often do you feel as though you're in the present moment during your golf game? How often do you experience this kind of focus in other areas of your life? Does your awareness remain on what you are doing? Or does it drift off to fictional times and places?

Score	Explanation	Example
Eagle	You are the Bruce Lee of presence.	You remember every name and every conversation you had at the speed-dating event.
Birdie	You stay in the now more than not.	Put aside your sadness that your dog just died so you could give that inspirational speech to kids.
Par	Sometimes you are present. Other times you are not.	You turned off your phone and enjoyed every second of your daughter's recital. As soon as it was over you checked your Facebook feed to see if you missed anything.
Bogey	Staying present remains elusive.	Distraction by worries of tomorrow's meeting caused you to rear end an old lady in the mall parking lot.
Double Bogey	Fear and anxiety render you useless.	You had a panic attack at the party and Suzy left with someone else while you were in the bathroom collecting yourself.

Score _____

Pro Tip

Please do yourself a favor and read *The Power of Now* by Eck-hart Tolle. Of all of the best spiritual, personal growth books I've ever read, it's perhaps the most important one I've read. It's hard to describe how clearly Tolle explains the truth about existence, which is that nothing is real except the moment you are in when you are in it. It will help you develop the awareness around the subject that you need in order to remain fully present on and off of the course.

Practice Drills

• *Double Bogey* • The next time you start freaking out about something that has already happened or something that might happen, stop yourself, take a deep breath and realize that none of those things are happening right NOW. Continue to focus on your breath and bring your awareness back to the present moment. Look around and connect to your surroundings and what is happening right NOW.

• *Bogey* • The next time you have a long drive in your car, challenge yourself to not allow your boredom to cause you to make 10 phone calls or obsess about what already happened today or will happen tonight. Instead turn up the music, sing along and enjoy the ride!

• *Par* • During your next round of golf, focus on bringing all of your consciousness to the millisecond of impact as it is happening. Nothing else matters at that moment except getting the club to strike the ball perfectly.

Hole 7

Play It As
It Lies

*"Golf's ultimate moral instruction directs us to find
within ourselves a pivotal center of enjoyment: relax
into a rhythm that fits in the hill and swales, and play the
shot at hand – not the last one, or the next one but the one
at your feet, in the poison ivy, where you put it."*
— John Updike

Everything changes in the instant that follows after the ball leaves the clubface. At this point, we no longer have control over where the ball will land. It will go where it goes and our job is quite simple. Go and find it. Then figure out what the next shot will be. Every time I do this, I learn the lesson of acceptance. It would be a waste of energy to lament a bad break. Whether the ball trickled into a bunker or you were recently laid off from a job. The lesson is the same.

It's tempting to look back and think about what we could have done differently. It's easy to complain to the golf gods, and moan, 'Why did this happen to me?' But doing this would be wasted energy. Why you? Why not you? None of our complaints will change what is so, either on or off the golf course. It merely distracts us from accepting what is so and then deciding what the best course of action is moving forward.

We've all seen people expend incredible amounts of time and energy talking about how things should have worked out differently.

- ♦ "I didn't deserve that bad bounce into the water."
- ♦ "My ex-girlfriend shouldn't have broken up with me during a time like this."
- ♦ "The group in front of us is playing too slow."
- ♦ "I should be paid a higher wage for what I do."

Whatever the exact details of the scenario, I'm guessing that most of us have also experienced these kinds of feelings. They are universal and I don't pretend to have a solution for them. However, it's important to realize that these thoughts take us out of the present moment, and drag us back into the past - a place where we have no control.

This is a concept I struggled with for a long time in golf. When I was playing poorly, I would use Mulligans, which is a golf term for taking a second chance to perform an action, after the first chance went wrong through bad luck or a blunder. Friends would often tease me about my liberal use of Mulligans. Even after my swing change, I would justify improving my lie by telling myself that I needed to get my swing down with good lies before I could learn to use it with whatever lie I was dealt. During this period of my life I was fighting acceptance in my career, in some important relation-ships, and other key areas. I worked on all of this both on and off the course for years, but when I wrote this book, it started to become clear that I had to live my life and play the game by the letter of the law, because doing otherwise would make me the guy who talks the talk, but doesn't walk the walk. We'll get further into the concept and practice of integrity on the 12th hole. For now, what I want to impress upon you is that I learned everything starts with accepting what is so. I'm not saying we have to like it, but I am saying that I had to find a way to embrace it.

In those early morning hours, with the mist still rising off of the greens, I kept replaying my own life. Self-examination can be healthy, but if can also become a distraction, and once again golf was there to show me the way. Play the shot that is at your feet - not the one you wish we had. All you can con-trol is what's in front of you right now. Start with acceptance of what lies in front of you, whatever that may be. Whether it's a plugged lie in a bunker or a car that rear-ended you last week, it is what it is. Now it's time to decide how to move forward. We can curse our 'bad luck' in either situation and even get people to agree with us about how it's terrible and we 'got screwed'. What will any of this really accomplish? I don't have the answers for everyone, but I do have the questions to ask. I'm just telling you that it helped me to say to myself, "This is what is so. What then is the best way forward? What can I learn from this? What opportunities did this create that weren't here before?"

Some might say, "How the heck does a 'bad' break create opportunities?!" The events in my life aren't good or bad, at least not until I attach an interpretation to them. This is how I started seeing 'the breaks' as just that... breaks. We examine the green and hit a strong putt, but the ball is not our friend, not in this moment. It does not break the way we expect that it will. Great athletes learn from these moments. They view hardship as an opportunity to grow. If the events of one's life are breaking the wrong way, try to see the opportunity that may be a natural byproduct of the scenario. It may be that bad luck has created a window or opportunity. The end of a relationship means there is new freedom to consider new experiences. The end of a job is the opportunity for reinvention of oneself and the opportunity to consider a new career. The more I think about this concept, the easier it becomes to watch the ball fade away from its intended target. Each new shot offers wisdom, experience, and the chance to learn as I make my way through the course.

Let's look at an example that might happen during a round of golf. I have a couple of specific examples from my past that are still clear as day so many years later. About 15 years ago, while playing on a bright, sunny day at a beautiful tree-lined course in Massachusetts, I pulled a driver left into the thick of the trees. I went to look for my ball with not much hope of finding it, but to my surprise not only did I find it, but it was sitting up on a good lie on some pine straw. As I looked toward the green I decided that I was about the distance it takes me to hit a 7-iron. I didn't have much to look at. I still had to make my way through the trees. Then I looked up. Holy crap. There was a tiny window above the trees, a portal through the canopy. If only I could hit my perfect 7-iron. I would need to account for the height of the opening, open up the club face and add some loft to the shot. My ball would have to follow the highest possible trajectory. Since I didn't really have another good option, I thought, 'what the heck?' So, I steadied myself, and committed to the shot. And don't you know, I hit one of the best shots I can remember. After the purest contact the ball soared over the trees and landed 10 feet from the pin. Predictably I missed the birdie putt. I was probably still too focused on how great a shot I had just hit. The walk out of the trees and onto the green was effortless. I practically floated there. And then I didn't see the putt at my feet. I was still high on the 7-iron I'd hit. Still, at that time in my life, I was pretty lucky to get out of there with a par after that tee shot.

On another occasion, just a few years ago while playing the 10th hole at Wayland Country Club in Massachusetts, I hooked my 3 wood into the trees on a dog-leg left where my ideal landing spot would've been right of right. Not good. As it was late fall, there were no leaves on the trees but hundreds of branches between my ball and the hole. I could have come out sideways or backwards but it would have taken a really good shot to create a good angle from the fairway to the hole. So I called my friend over and said, 'Hey, I have no shot. Watch this." I took a 9 iron and put the ball in the back of my stance to hit a low punch. I made a great swing and caught the ball exactly as I wanted to, but with all the shrubbery in front of me, it was up to the golf gods now. The ball appeared to move in slow motion through the air, like a bullet whistling through the fight scene of a Hollywood thriller. I imagined myself as Neo from *The Matrix*, making *Kung Fu* gestures as my ball narrowly avoided each branch along its flight path. It clipped the very last branch, and popped up into the air eventually coming to rest just 4 feet from the hole. This time I made the birdie putt - probably the best, and luckiest birdie I've ever made.

We've all hit bad shots. I used to beat myself up about it. Other golfers might blame the poor swing they were taught to use, or blame the bad shot on any number of possible distractions. This initial reaction is natural. It can be hard to control your emotions. What we can control is how quickly we let that go and reset our intention. Disengage and step back to take a moment. Reset our intentions and move forward. Golfers know that there is no better feeling than hitting a shot that is above one's ability, a shot we shouldn't be able to make. Golfers love it when shots like these make a round fall into place. What is needed is to hit that shot to par a difficult hole and it actually happens.

Think about some of the most epic shots that Tiger Woods ever hit in his professional career. Many of them came after terrible drives or really 'bad breaks' that resulted in a poor lie.

Had he not hit those poor drives or gotten those 'bad breaks,' those historic shots would have never occurred.

Then there's other times where you just simply get a 'bad break' and nothing good seems to come of it. It just hurts. It's a hard lesson. You may recall the shot that Tiger hit at the 15th hole in the 2nd round of the 2013 Masters. Sitting in the middle of the fairway, he launched an absolute dart at the hole. Unfortunately for him it was a bulls-eye and hit the pin squarely shooting the ball into the water. Instead of a 1 or 2 foot birdie putt that would have put him in first place and set him up for another potential major win, he made bogey, lost some critical momentum and ended up finishing T4...ironically watching his former caddy help another player, Adam Scott, to his first major win. A bitter lesson indeed.

Many times it takes courage to accept what is. Like anything, it takes practice and repetition to find the courage to move forward when we feel that things just haven't worked out the way we envisioned. Yet there is always a way forward from where we are...even if it's not that way we hoped for.

I'm no stranger to bad breaks, and these hard times have taught me that life is also a game of inches. The slightest thing can bring you great joy or pain, depending on how you choose to view it. Yet we can't forget the truth that all moments are gifts, especially the tough ones. The challenges help us to grow and become better golfers and people. We must learn to live in the moments that we have instead of living in the moments that we wish we had. We cannot control the past or the future. We can only control the shot at our feet.

Ask yourself, are you accepting what is so or are you fighting it and wishing things were different?

Score	Explanation	Example
Eagle	Acceptance is 2nd nature to you.	Your flight home got cancelled so you went on another adventure where you met the love of your life.
Birdie	You are accepting except one area of your life.	You are cool with everything, but why does your girlfriend have to put your entire relationship on Facebook?
Par	You know where you have trouble with acceptance and correct it.	You got pissed off they forgot the cheese on your sandwich. Then realized this helped your diet.
Bogey	Resistance usually wins out over acceptance.	You can't sleep because the neighbor's dog is barking again. Ear plugs anyone?
Double Bogey	You resist everything with a fury.	You can't enjoy the game because the announcer's voice is too nasally.

Score _____

Pro Tip

Resisting acceptance is akin to swimming upstream in a raging river. It is generally fruitless and utterly exhausting. Identify areas in your life where you are resisting what is so and write them down in a list so you can clearly see them as named obstacles that you have created. Then learn to live with those things so that you can put your energy toward governing yourself accordingly based on your commitments rather than wasting that energy resisting what cannot be changed.

Practice Drills

• *Double Bogey* • Write yourself an email about 3 things you are resisting in life. Don't hold back in complaining about and explaining why all of these things are unfair. When you then receive the email from yourself think about what you would say if this was your friend complaining to you about things they can't control. This should provide some perspective on how ridiculous it sounds.

• *Bogey* • The next time something happens to you that you can't accept, just walk away from it and let it go. Instead of dwelling on it, go help a friend or a stranger with something else, even if it's something trivial. Doing things for others is a great way to let go of your personal pity party.

• *Par* • Go to your local practice facility or play a round on an empty course. Purposefully give yourself horrible lies so you can practice what it is like to play the ball no matter where it is.

Hole 8

Grinding And Thriving

"Golf can give you so much joy and make you want to punch yourself in the head all in the same day"
— Marc Leishman

Golf can often appear to be a seesaw act between grinding and thriving. We are grinding when nothing seems to work. A round seems more like a death march. The ball will find the beach, or the water, or the clubhouse and a bowl of soup. We are thriving when the opposite is true. Everything seems to flow. We barely have to try and the ball just seems to carry over the obstacles that seem almost humorously insignificant. We reach the green in two. We stride confidently into the clubhouse, and the soup is delicious.

The truth is that both thriving and grinding are important pieces of the puzzle. It would be boring if we were always thriving, which is a much more difficult concept to digest than how exhausting it would be if we were constantly grinding. Having both of these experiences makes for a well-rounded journey filled with important lessons. The practice of patience allows me to let things be as they are without allowing frustration to blind me. I can then enjoy the roller coaster ride as it happens.

No two golf rounds are the same. No two days on this earth are the same. Sometimes it seems as is the stars themselves have aligned in our favor. We're content with our career, family, friends and everything just seems to flow naturally and smoothly. Not coincidentally these are often the times when this same smooth flow tends to present itself during a round of golf. We've all had those days where, for no apparent reason, we're seeing and executing the shot almost effortlessly and every putt seems destined for the bottom of the cup. Alternatively, I am guessing that I'm not the only person who has felt like the Universe itself is working against me. Please tell me I'm not alone. It's happened to you too, right? A day in which you just can't find the rhythm, no matter what you try.

Nothing seems go right and there doesn't seem to be anything you can do about it.

This concept reminds me of a Scottsdale golf trip some friends and I took in the spring of 2010. We were to play 5 rounds in 3 days at Desert Mountain Golf Club, which features 6 Jack Nicklaus designed courses in the most gorgeous desert setting you've ever seen. Somewhere in the middle of the trip I took to referring to this place as 'golf heaven.' When you play that much golf in that short of a period of time, it really drills home the idea that no two shots (and certainly no two rounds) are quite the same. Another insight gleaned from playing on 5 different Nicklaus courses within 72 hours is that the same hole can offer completely different views and challenges to the same player.

The first day we had an early tee time on the Cochise course on a perfect morning. The sun was shining, there wasn't a breath of wind, the views were stunning and the desert animals were doing their dance. It was literally a picture perfect setting. The conditions could not have been better, so of course I played like crap. I was like a bird turd on the Rolls Royce of courses and I didn't break 100. After lunch we went to the other side of the property to play the Outlaw course. The skies had become overcast, the wind was whipping, and they had let the grass die in preparation for some upcoming landscaping project. It could not have been a more different experience in terms of playing conditions. All we did was walk across the property and suddenly it felt like we were in another country. For whatever reason, I played great that afternoon in much tougher conditions and carded something like an 86. In fact, at one point I hit a drive so well that it traveled just over 300 yards (downhill and downwind), which is something I've only done on one other occasion. Of course my playing partner had to show me up by absolutely destroying his tee shot, and sending the ball 400 yards down the fairway on the same hole!

In one day I had had two radically different experiences. What could I learn from this? How should I react when thriving? What should I do if I find myself grinding? We just never know when things are going to go smoothly or when we're going to be challenged, so the best thing we can do is be ready for whatever comes our way and adjust accordingly.

I decided that when grinding, the most appropriate choice one can make (when nothing appears to be going well) is to focus on patience. Challenges will continue to show up until we learn the lessons they are here to deliver. Not only is it the whole point – to learn and grow through tough times, but it also gives us perspective so that we truly get to soak in and enjoy the amazing times.

Without the difficulties, both life and golf would be boring. Think about it. If everything went our way all the time, that would just be the norm so it would technically be the same all the time - not good or bad but the same old, same old. Even if that same old is all the stuff we really love, eventually our love for those things is diminished due to overexposure.

Looking at it in the context of golf, constant thriving would be akin to hitting every fairway, hitting every green and making every putt. Yes, it sounds fantastic at first. I mean who wouldn't want to shoot -38 in one round like Kim Jong Il reportedly did at the ripe old age of 54?! But seriously, if we birdied every hole every time we played, it would get monotonous, although I'll admit it might take a while. The point is that if success were all we knew, it would be mundane. The fun comes from the challenge of trying to do the best we can at a really difficult game. Problems make life interesting and errant shots are the golf gods way of telling us that this is going to be a fascinating day on the links.

Every day I try to accept that challenges are inevitable and necessary for growth. Some days and rounds are going to be better than others. But if I resist and cling to what I want, nothing changes. I merely fill my day with more pain and frustration. In the words of Thom York, "You do it to yourself, and that's what really hurts." In golf, we grind and grind and choose to be miserable. We want to shrug it off and carry on. And then another ball helps to prune the vegetation.

Who can forget Rory McIlroy's meltdown at the 2011 Masters? The rising young star had the Sunday lead on the 10th tee and he was inching closer to the first major championship of his career. Then he pulled his tee shot into the cabins way left of the fairway. From there the wheels fell off and he was not able to recover. This paved the way for Charl Schwartzel, who won his first major championship.

Rory was a good sport about the whole thing and kept working at his game, grinding away through the tour season and preparing for his next shot at a major, which would come at the U.S. Open hosted at Congressional CC in mid June. He was ready and took a 3 shot lead after day one. Fans and pundits wondered aloud whether Rory would be able to hold a lead this time. McIlroy left no doubt as he stretched the lead to six shots after two rounds and ended up blowing the field away by eight shots to win his first major. Winning any championship is great, and an example of thriving, but one must admit, the win was made much sweeter following Rory's collapse at Augusta. He could have lost his patience and wallowed in sorrow and doubt for months, or even years after such a heart-breaking loss. But instead he chose to accept the challenge in front of him and to use the experience as motivation to get better. We all have that choice whenever presented with a frustration.

Rory has another notable grinding example in his professional career, and once again it teaches us the value of patience in the face of hardship. It's important to remember that this guy is known to have one of the purest swings and to be one of the best ball strikers in the world. I recently learned that it took McIlroy 522 professional rounds of golf before he made his first hole in one. Even with a swing like his it took him nearly 2,100 chances to drop one in the hole (during tournament play). As good as he is, that is just astonishing.

Another very relatable example for golfers is when we seem to get everything clicking and we've played a good round, perhaps for the first time in a while. Next time we go play, it's just not the same and we've slightly regressed rather than progressed. For professionals, we often see how hard it is to put together a good round after a really low round flirting with 60. Sometimes, there's not even an explanation as to why this happens. It's just a reminder that all moments - good or bad - are fleeting.

This type of perspective creates an attitude necessary for 'weathering the storms' when they come. We can take a step back and try to figure out what the lesson is because we are present to the moment that is happening - instead of the one we wish was happening. We can also remind ourselves that nothing is permanent and this challenge too shall pass. Viewing things in this manner reinforces our patience, keeping us from getting discouraged and restoring our faith that better days and better rounds are ahead. Conversely, we should also remember that the great shots and great moments too shall pass. This teaches us to soak up every moment of glory; these times are fleeting. Such is life. Such is golf.

Are you remaining humble and graceful, well aware that soon enough turbulent times will return? Or will you continue to resist the natural vacillation between grinding and thriving on and off the course?

Score	Explanation	Example
Eagle	Taking wins and losses in perfect stride is how you roll.	You broke your arm so you decided to teach yourself how to write and putt with your left hand.
Birdie	You stay mostly stable during good or bad times.	You hit on a scratch ticket for $10k, paid off credit card and gave the rest to charity.
Par	Tough times are challenging but at least you can find some silver lining.	That blizzard caused you to miss a big gig. At least you finally got to read War and Peace.
Bogey	Life's ebbs and flows are getting the best of you.	You were so mad that your back was out again that your anger caused you to miss the massage that your wife had booked for you.
Double Bogey	The roller coaster ride is driving you crazy.	You had a nervous breakdown because it rained 5 days in a row.

Score _____

Pro Tip

This is a good chance to work on being non-judgmental with yourself or others. Remind yourself that situations, challenges or even gifts aren't necessarily good or bad until you attach your interpretation to them. Keep in mind that your interpretation is completely fabricated – by you! Why not create an interpretation that serves you instead of one that victimizes you? You can get so good at this that you completely strip away interpretation from challenges or benefits that come your way. This paves the way for emotional stability no matter what gets thrown at you.

Practice Drills

• *Double Bogey* • The first thing to do is to identify when you are being impatient. Pay attention this week and make a list of all the times you lose your patience. It doesn't matter if it's a big or small upset. Just pay attention. It might surprise you how often you are choosing misery.

• *Bogey* • The next step after becoming aware of your impatience is exploring how it affects you. After you've made your list of the times you've been impatient, then make a new one where you write down how the impatience in each scenario made you feel. How did you feel mentally AND physically when impatience was happening?

• *Par* • Now start to practice patience. The next time you're in a hurry and stuck in a grocery check out line (or any similar situation), acknowledge that your impatience has kicked in. Take a deep breath to alleviate the mental and physical symptoms that are arising. Now you can choose patience. Push yourself to GENUINELY smile at the person that is holding up the line and say something truly kind or silly to them.

Hole 9

Lost And Found

"Pain and suffering are inevitable in our lives,
but misery is an option."
— Chip Beck

This life is a gift. This game of golf is also a gift. We should never forget this, no matter what happens. Sometimes, at the end of the front nine, I feel like I have been endlessly grinding and absolutely nothing is working. In my personal life, there just seems to be nothing but challenge after challenge at work and at home. It's frustrating beyond belief and it can leave a person feeling lost. Golf has taught me that when this happens I have a choice. I can wallow in my woes and quit. Or I can keep the faith and remember that this is all part of the play that I signed up for.

In golf that lost feeling occurs as a sensation. We suddenly have this feeling that we've never swung a club before, and absolutely nothing is comfortable. It usually leads to thoughts about why we even bother playing this dumb game. It was supposed to be fun and relaxing and now it's just infuriating and exhausting. My dad likes to mentally prepare himself for his inevitable mental breakdown in a round by proclaiming the following self-fulfilling prophecy of doom on the first tee box. "Let the torture begin!" he'll say. Although not recommended in the list of pre-round routines, it always gets a chuckle because we've all been there.

Like a long challenging round of golf, feeling lost in one's daily life is usually preceded by a number of things happening in quick succession. I'm talking about events that challenge our core beliefs. We meet someone who doesn't play much and they are clearly better than us. A long day at the course culminates in a shot that makes one feel terrible about himself. And we say something like, "Of course that would happen." A setback in life causes us to doubt our original plans.

Maybe I shouldn't have tried to become successful as a banker, a lawyer, a doctor, or an architect. We think, "Maybe I'm not cut out for this."

Allow me to paraphrase an old adage; *we can't see the golf course for the trees*. This is when it's most important to keep the faith. And with regard to faith, I'm not necessarily talking about spiritual faith. To me F.A.I.T.H. translates to Fostering Awareness In The Heart. It's a similar concept to what was discussed on the 4th hole. When negative thoughts are buzzing around one's brain at lightning speed, the best way to slow things down is to stop and breathe. When we do that, we can eventually slow down enough to start to choose our thoughts from a deeper, wiser place.

One of my best friends struggles mightily with this concept on and off of the golf course. Not coincidentally his surname is Mulligan, which for those who don't know is golf's synonym for 'do-over'. I remember a time on a warm winter day in Florida when he was spraying the ball all over the place. On hole after hole he kept digging his own holes in the ground with furious swings. On the 9th hole he was about 50 yards out and proceeded to dig down and hit behind the ball throwing huge divots in his wake like some Three Stooges golf episode. Within a matter of what seemed like seconds, he took 5 shots to get his ball on the green. He kept doing the same thing over and over, and wondering why things didn't get better. On this particular day, he decided to ask for help when he finally made it onto on the green.

Better late than never. My brother-in-law kindly stepped in and gave him a tip, which led him to making much better contact for the rest of the round.

When we are lost it is important to take a moment to step back and realize that we need to ask for help. Asking for assistance is not an admission that there is something wrong with us. It's merely an acknowledgement of our humanity. None of us are perfect, and we all need outside help at times.

Feeling lost is something that everyone endures. Let's look at the example of Padraig Harrington, who, after winning 3 majors, decided to do what he had always done...tinker with his swing. After tinkering commenced, it wasn't long before Padraig began to plummet down the world rankings. He's a great golfer, but it's likely that even he would admit that he went through an awful professional period where he just couldn't seem to find the right swing. Many questioned his decisions, and I'm ashamed to admit that I was one of them. Then I learned that this is what he had always done, and that 'tinkering' remains an important part of who he is. In staying true to himself he may have cost himself some money and trophies, but he never lost faith in himself as a person or a golfer. Although I've met Padraig a couple of times, I don't know him and I don't know that he never lost faith. Although I recently saw an interview on Golf Channel where he did say that no matter what has happened, as his confidence rose or fell, he has always kept his underlying belief in himself and his ability. This was proven true in the past couple of years, as we've seen him rise once again in the world rankings, winning a tournament and contending in many others.

I don't want to go too deep into spirituality or religion in this book, but a really good example of what to do when we feel lost is to remember the words of the old hymnal, Amazing Grace. "I once was lost, but now I'm found. Was blind, but now I see." Looking at this from a purely secular view, what it's saying is that when we are lost we can't see why we are being challenged so deeply. Then at some point - sometimes many days or years later - we realize what the lesson was and why we had to go through it.

Feeling lost without being able to calm down and see the big picture can also lead to actions with serious and permanent repercussions. On the course we can throw a club and hurt someone, curse out the club pro or toss our clubs in the basement and never play again. Of course no one in their right mind wants to hurt another person. Nor do we want to get kicked out of our favorite club because we lost our temper. And although quitting might seem to alleviate the anguish in the short term, it also robs us of the joy we get during the good times playing the game we love.

There is a course I like to occasionally play. It's become familiar over the years, like your favorite hiking trail on the mountain. But knowing a course can only help you so much when you are lost. I remember losing several balls on this course on a day in early May. The last one I lost was the most vexing, because I could swear that I'd seen where it landed. Only when I arrived at the spot I'd picked out in the tee box, the ball was nowhere to be seen. I searched and searched and after a few minutes I could tell that the other players were getting impatient. Giving up on that ball felt like a big choice, as if I was giving up on myself. I had to find it. A few more minutes passed and nothing changed. Walking out of that crops of trees I felt weary and dejected. My Titleist with a scratch in the third dimple just above the logo was gone.

It had been my lucky ball, and now I was a man unmoored from his own history. The years of practice and the confidence I'd built up were all gone. After a few weeks my confidence slowly began to return, and then several months later I played the course again. Like a bad reoccurring dream I hit the same slice into the trees to the right of the fairway and there it was, months later, the Titleist with the scratch just sitting behind a small rock. When I tell you that an irrational belief in my abilities returned, you will find me a little ridiculous. It's just a ball. It has nothing to do with my skill level. And yet it was only in finding it that I could summon the perspective to see this. I had no need for a lucky ball. It was me. It was always me.

Through intense pain comes the most growth. It must be said that sometimes we just need to work on our pain tolerance and it is completely okay to ask for help with that. Whatever it is you're are going through, there is always a way forward if you are willing to be tough enough to search for it.

This life is not easy for any of us. It doesn't matter if we are rich, poor, white, black, gay, straight, male or female. We all have incredible challenges to face that can leave us filled with despair. And golf is not an easy game. Whether one is a zero handicap or a 30 handicap, she will miss shots and get discouraged. So remain faithful, and remember that we are always on our path – whether we like it or not. It is literally impossible to be anywhere else. So hang in there and ask for help. We're all in this mess together! The more we act like it, the more we can help each other in this crazy game.

How are you doing in life and golf? Are you keeping the faith? Do you feel good or do you feel lost?

Score	Explanation	Example
Eagle	You have the FAITH of Mother Theresa.	You know that failing the bar exam 4 times is going to lead you to something great eventually.
Birdie	You mostly see the big picture.	You haven't had sex with your wife in 3 weeks but bring home flowers because you love her any-way (and maybe tonight is the night!)
Par	You waiver between faith and anger.	You love your family and friends but on your Face-book page you only post negative/ divisive stories.
Bogey	You are mostly hope-less with glimmers of hope now and again.	You lost due to bad luck for the 7th straight week at your poker game. Your friends must be cheating you.
Double Bogey	You want to quit because it's just not worth it.	After another bad round of golf you threw your entire golf bag in the lake and told off your friends.

Score _____

Pro Tip

When you feel lost you have to find a way to step outside of the pain and struggle so you can stop your negative thoughts, pulling you further down into a dangerous rabbit hole. The simplest action to take in moments of great despair is to focus on your breath. You literally bring all awareness to your breathing and attempt to shut everything else out. Just a few minutes of this can help dramatically. Another trick that has worked well for me is to actually say 'stop' or 'reset' out loud to myself in attempt to gain control of the runaway train of negative messages running through my head. Try these next time you feel lost.

Practice Drills

• *Double Bogey* • The next time you feel lost, remove yourself from the situation and do something nice for yourself that grounds you. Some options may be going for a hike in a beautiful place, going to a nice beach to sit and look at the water or getting a massage. Just pick something that you enjoy and which will remind you that all is not lost no matter how bad it seems.

• *Bogey* • Take a few moments and write down all of the things you are thankful for in your life. Then put those in a prominent place where you will see them daily (bathroom mirror, refrigerator, etc). This helps you focus on the things that will keep you moving forward

• *Par* • Ask for help. Whether you're dealing with a personal issue or something in your golf game that you just can't get past, ask for help getting clarity on the situation from a friend or a professional. It is not bad to ask for help!!

Making the Turn

Like stopping at the snack shack at the turn to refuel after completing the first half of your golf round, it will be just as beneficial for us to have a mental snack here as we regroup and get ready to attack the back nine of this book. Let's tally our score and review some key points from the outward nine holes:

Hole 1 ★ Swing Your Swing – Looking deeply inward to uncover the best version of ourselves on and off of the golf course.

Score _____

Hole 2 ★ Practice Doesn't Make Perfect – Learning to practice things that actually help you uncover your best and deliver the results that you desire.

Score _____

Hole 3 ★ Confidence Is Key – Learning to access your most confident self as often as possible.

Score _____

Hole 4 ★ Mind Games - Learning to quiet your mind in order to obtain a clean slate so you can focus and create the things you want.

Score _____

Hole 5 ★ Re:Vision - Learning the practice of visualizing or imagining the things that you want to manifest.

Score _____

Hole 6 ★ The Moment Of Impact - Learning to stay present in the current moment so that you can put all of your energy into 'the moment of impact.'

Score _____

Hole 7 ★ Play It As It Lies - Learning the practice of acceptance so you can deal with things as they are, instead of lamenting about how you wish they were.

Score _____

Hole 8 ★ Grinding And Thriving – Learning the practice of patience so daily frustrations can't derail you.

Score _____

Hole 9 ★ Lost And Found – Learning the practice of F.A.I.T.H. so we can see the big picture and remember that this too shall pass.

Score _____

Front 9 Total Score To Par _____

Hole 10

Timing Is Everything

"You don't have the game you played last week. You only have today's game. It may be far from your best, but that's all you've got. Harden your heart and make the best of it."
— Walter Hagen

Timing in a golf swing is crucial. Without timing, it's impossible to hit the ball squarely. Repetition and practice will help but it can't be forced. Timing is either there or it's not. It is the same throughout the rest of our lives. We can try to speed things up and 'make things happen', but this will often lead to frustration. There is an art to achieving the balance necessary to know when to allow things to happen and when to ratchet up the effort level. Many times we end up going from one extreme to the other.

Before we go any further, I want to be clear that I'm not suggesting that we sit back and let life happen to us. There are often benefits to being driven and proactive. What I'm are talking about is making sure to be aware enough to know the difference between forging ahead in a productive manner and losing patience, which leads to forcing a situation, and ultimately, to being the precise factor that prevents the desired outcome from occurring.

Not to discount confidence and determination, because they are absolutely critical to a good golf game and a fulfilling life. Yet if they go unchecked they can lead to disaster. Sometimes we have to take things as they come and deal with what's in front of us, rather than trying to push through adversity by overreacting to what just happened and trying to 'make up ground' because we made a mistake.

Golf fans will never forget Jean Van de Velde's epic collapse at the 1999 Open Championship at Carnoustie. He was leading the tournament as he stood on the tee of the 72nd hole, and he only needed a double bogey to become the first French born major champion. He chose to unnecessarily hit a driver off the tee, which he put right down the middle. It was a questionable choice but he got away with it. He was not so fortunate with his next shot. All he had to do was hit back-to-back wedge shots and then three putt his way to a victory. Instead he chose to hit a fairway wood, which hit the grandstand and ricocheted into the deep rough. No worries. All he had to do now was chop it out to a safe place, chip it onto the green and 2 putt for the win. Unfortunately, he wanted more than a safe limp across the finish line. So he cursed the bad lie that caused him to hit it into the creek that protected the green. He almost played it out of the water but chose more wisely, albeit a bit late for sound reasoning. Even now, he could still win if he would just hit the ball onto the green and make the following putt. Sadly, he hit it in the greenside bunker and needed to make it from there. He did not but, did make the putt to get into a three-way playoff that he lost. Poor decision-making led to compounded errors and forced shots. Van de Velde is now remembered for the greatest collapse in golf history instead of being the only French major champion.

Once, while on a golf trip in Ireland, I was playing at Old Head Golf Links, which is playfully referred to as 'the Pebble Beach of Ireland.' While playing, I noticed that I was forcing every swing and compounding every prior poor swing by trying to get it all back on the next swing. This only made things worse and worse as the round went on. I just couldn't relax enough to get out of my own way. I became increasingly tense and agitated about my swing. Finally, somewhere on the 14th hole, my hilarious Irish caddie couldn't take it any longer and quipped, "For f#@k sake lad, just make a swing. What's the worst that could happen?" He had had it with me – and quite frankly, so had I. I decided he was right and committed to letting go and just making a free, unforced swing on the next shot. Predictably I hit it right on the nose. I wish he said that to me on the 3rd hole!

Many of us have experienced firsthand how frustrating and exhausting it can be to try and force the right swing to happen. I can say from firsthand experience that going against the flow of the Universe is a losing and draining battle. This is the exact reason why I gave up my career in the entertainment business - because it was exhausting and unfulfilling. It is much easier to be balanced when going with the flow and seeing where the journey takes you. Imagine the metaphor of a stream or river. Swimming against the current is almost futile, while letting the current gently steer you downstream and flowing along the way is quite effortless and natural. That's not to say that you have no control when flowing with the current. You can stop or divert your course along the way. This is the metaphor of free will.

With regard to a non-forced golf swing, there probably hasn't been a finer example than Ernie Els. It is for good reason that he is often referred to as 'The Big Easy.' No one is perfect and Ernie as a golfer is no exception. Having said that, his timing is perfect. There is not one thing forced about his swing. It is free and smooth and he achieves the exact same tempo every single time he swings a club. As someone who has continually struggled with timing and tempo in their golf swing, I marvel at how easily his swing flows and how repeatable it is. If you look at video of Els in 2000 and now in 2018, you'll see no difference in that 'easy' swing.

Almost none of us are ever going to play at the level of Ernie Els and I'm not suggesting that any of us try to copy his swing. I believe you should swing *your* swing. At the same time, there is certainly value in visualizing and emulating his timing and tempo as you practice and play. You can also keep the image of Els' swing in our minds as you go through your everyday life. The next time you sense that you are forcing something, and swimming against the tide, remember that swing.

Whether I'm on the golf course or in the office, there is intrinsic value in mastering the balance between forcing things and letting them come to me naturally. I'm constantly trying to remember to let life take me where it will, while simultaneously remaining aware enough to impose a touch of free will here and there. This is the way to direct our own course without disrupting the overall flow, and without draining ourselves by constantly fighting against that Universal flow.

Are you forcing things in your life or golf swing? Or are you letting them flow organically?

Score	Explanation	Example
Eagle	You are a Flow Master.	You always punch out from the trees and set yourself up for the next shot.
Birdie	You rarely force things with minor exceptions.	You celebrate and foster individuality in your family – but you insist on matching sweaters on the Christmas card.
Par	To flow or not to flow?	You let your friends plan your birthday party but you tell them when to sing – and in what key.
Bogey	You generally try to make things happen instead of let them happen.	Determined to MAKE anti-social Andy in accounting like you.
Double Bogey	You are a battering ram of forcing things and wonder why you're so miserable.	Bridezilla on the hunt for storybook wedding at all costs, is how you do life.

Score _____

Pro Tip

When I find myself forcing something, I like to do a similar exercise to what I suggested at the end of the last hole. Telling yourself to 'stop' or 'reset' can create a space that allows you to bring faith and freedom to your swing or your life. I also like visualizing a river and reminding myself that I have a choice to swim against the current or let it take me where it will. In that context, it's difficult to make the exhausting and frustrating choice to force things that aren't meant to be.

Practice Drills

◆ *Double Bogey* ◆ Sign-up for a tai chi or yoga class. Both of these incorporate the physical practice of flow along with the mental and spiritual, but start with the physical practice as it's an easier one to grasp for those who are constantly resisting flow.

◆ *Bogey* ◆ Go to a large farmer's market and commit to staying in the flow of the people you encounter as well as the food and other products. There are some amazing people and cuisines that can be found at these events. It's a great place to practice flow.

◆ *Par* ◆ Take a day trip by yourself or with a companion. The only rule is that you don't get to plan anything. Just start heading in a direction and see where the trip takes you and who you encounter along the way. You can use maps and Google. Just don't plan anything ahead of time and pay attention so that you can remain open to any twists and turns the flow throws your way. I have had some amazing experiences traveling like this. This is the true practice of flow.

Hole 11

Body Of Work

"The biggest technological advance in golf in the next 50 years won't be equipment or exercise. It'll be nutrition."
— *Gary Player*

As I write this book, people in the United States and around the world are obtaining a heightened awareness about health and wellness. This is no doubt in part due to the availability of information. Today, social media and a 24-hour news cycle make us more informed than ever before. Many of us remember a time when we couldn't easily research a topic and find an answer within seconds. That's why in matters of health and wellness, people generally had to 'take someone's word for it.' One of the benefits of the information age is that we can now research our options and take control of our own health and well-being.

For all of Tiger Woods recent personal issues and health concerns, his long-term, positive influence on the game of golf cannot be denied. Bringing professional athletic-level health and wellness to the game of golf on a grand scale will undoubtedly be a part of his permanent legacy. Before Tiger came along, professional golf - save for Gary Player and a handful of others - was largely filled with beer-guzzling and cigarette-smoking couch potato types. Tiger showed the world how to take incredible natural ability, unmatched competitiveness - which many had before him - and combine it with an elite athletic body. His success illustrated that this combination could dominate the field if the golfer was physically and mentally ready for the challenge.

These days just about every professional golfer and millions of amateur golfers take health, wellness, and fitness very seriously. There just simply aren't that many John Dalys left in the game of golf. Professional golf is now filled with men and women who are elite athletes. Golfers like Dustin Johnson, Brooks Koepka and Lexi Thompson exemplify this change. As a result, amateur golfers all over the planet are following suit and paying more attention to eating right, working out, and getting proper rest.

Whether for reasons of playing better golf, or for our own personal non-golf-related well-being, taking care of our bodies should be a priority for each and every one of us. Our bodies are the vessels through which we experience life. Without a healthy body - brain, muscles, and organs - our ability to experience life to the fullest is severely diminished.

Although Tiger took fitness to new levels, Gary Player was really golf's patron saint of health and well-being. He was miles ahead of his contemporaries in this area, and he was teased and even downright ridiculed for his forward-thinking approach to fitness. Really he was the first one to see golfers as athletes, and he did this decades prior to Tiger Woods' emergence on the golf stage.

In the 50s and 60s, while others were drinking beer, smoking cigarettes and eating burgers, Player was eating salads and working out like a maniac. The man referred to as The Black Knight said, "I took an oath to God that I would never eat another piece of bacon or eat another ice cream in my life and I've adhered to it." That's pretty drastic, even by modern standards. It's no surprise that back then people thought he was nuts. He proved them wrong, however, by winning more than 150 tournaments and 9 majors worldwide.

For more proof that Player was way ahead of his time, look at the wellness regimens that current golfers go by today. They are based on the same concepts he saw over 50 years ago! Now in his 80s, The Black Knight still works out 4-5 times per week, doing core work and cardio. How evolved was Player's wellness philosophy for its time? Consider that it wasn't just about working out. It included a healthy diet and rest for the body.

The modern version of this philosophy is what has allowed other athletes like Tom Brady to excel at their sport well past a typical age. If improved health and wellness leads to more wins, then that's what you do. Our body is our temple.

In golf, just like anything else, we're no good to anyone if we're tired, hungry, and cranky. I've seen some incredible rounds of golf on little to no sleep, but that is the exception and not the rule.

I was in Vegas in the late 2000s with some good buddies. We were having a great 'Vegas' time eating, drinking and partying like pigs, which is fine – until our 8 am tee time came up. Now Cascata is probably the nicest courses in Las Vegas and one of the nicest in the U.S. and we had gotten on for free through a connection – a savings of $500+ in greens fees each. We're talking an amazing track with world-class facilities and staff, so of course we rewarded them by falling out of our cab still drunk on 1 hour of 'sleep'. I'll never forget standing in front of Jack Nicklaus' locker in awe of his great presence – while trying not to throw up.

Finally we make our way to the driving range where 2 out of the 3 of us literally almost fall over on the first swing. Luckily the staff there was amazing and delivered Bloody Marys and breakfast burritos to us on the driving range! I told you this place is world-class. I actually started the round playing fairly well until the hot desert sun kicked in and I think I shot a thousand that day. One of my buddies who is a special golfer had to show off and shoot 1 under that day. Of course these things are possible as one offs but not sustainable as a regular routine so best to leave them as a part of Vegas lore where they belong.

One of the worst things I've heard in recent years is the ridiculous phrase "work hard, play hard". We are not meant to go, go, go all of the time. We cannot be at our best if we are continually drained. The body needs rest. Our brains need rest. The body can heal and regenerate itself through rest via meditation or deep sleep. When we're going, going, going all the time we literally compromise everything we are working and playing for. One thing I've learned through writing this book is that I'm not very good at it if I'm not rested and grounded.

Also diet is a major concern in our society. Most people are systematically poisoning their bodies without knowing it. I once got paired with an older gentleman while walking a twilight round on the Wilson course in Griffith Park in Los Angeles. We chatted throughout the round and eventually I found out that he was a cardiac doctor at USC. What he told me about diet blew my mind. He said that in the 60s he and his colleagues were doing research that not only proved that the vegan diet slows the aging process, but it actually reverses it!! I'm not suggesting we should all become vegan. Yet I do believe that we would all be healthier if we did. What I am saying is that most of us aren't even close to eating healthy and we should try to do better.

Let's face it. We live in a toxic society. Much of our food and beverages are filled with sweeteners and chemicals. In public debate, the constant contention based on differing views, and our increasing dependence of technology and electronics, creates poisonous energy that get absorbed into our bodies. If that wasn't enough, the pharmaceutical industry wants us to take our 'medicine,' and though these chemicals can be helpful for some, there is ample evidence that they can also cause great harm. We must learn to seek natural wellness treatments and routines that draw these toxins out of our bodies to create a space for true health.

Are you paying enough attention to your health and wellness?

Score	Explanation	Example
Eagle	Gary Player would be proud or your diet and exercise program.	You gave up sugar – forever.
Birdie	You are on your way to perfect health.	You found a program that works for you and are diligently trying to stick to it.
Par	You are mostly healthy but neglecting some things.	You eat well and exercise regularly but only sleep 3 hours per night.
Bogey	Major health changes are still needed.	You started walking 3 times a week, but you still eat Taco Bell 5 times a week.
Double Bogey	Your wellness is a major concern.	My 600 lb Life is your favorite show because it makes you feel fit.

Score _____

Pro Tip

Eating right, drinking lots of water and getting 'real' rest is a good place to start. One size - or plan - does not fit all, and there is no magic pill or program. We must all commit to seeking our personal path to health and wellness. Again we must be honest with ourselves in order to do our absolute best to find what works for each of us. Also too much of a good thing can be harmful - over-exercising, drinking too much water, sleeping too much, etc. - so do your due diligence to find out what would be best for you. Above all be kind to yourself. If you can't be kind to yourself, how can you be kind to others?

Practice Drills

• *Double Bogey* • Join a gym or sign up for regular yoga or Pilates classes. Most health professionals agree that you should be exercising for at least 30 minutes, 3 times a week. This is the minimum.

• *Bogey* • Make healthy eating a priority. It's time to give up fast food, forever. Your body will thank you. Do some research, talk to your doctor and adopt an eating plan. I won't go so far as to say you should become vegan. I am not vegan. Although there's plenty of research that suggests that is the healthiest diet. You should definitely try to eat less processed foods and less refined sugars.

• *Par* • Make sure to get your rest! Not everyone needs 8 hours of sleep every night. Some need more and some need less. Stop kidding yourself that less is enough and make sure you get the sleep you need. Also turn off the TV at night! You should sleep in a cool, quiet, dark place to get complete rest. Supplemental meditation also helps a lot.

Hole 12

Jerk. Off.

"A bad attitude is worse than a bad golf swing."
— Payne Stewart

The title of this chapter is meant to be an attention grabber – because this is important. Let's talk about how to not be a jerk on the golf course. And while we're at it, let's talk about not being a jerk at home or in the office as well. Our goal in life is to be the best person we are capable of being - one day and one moment at a time. Paying taxes on time and petting the family dog once in a while doesn't get us off the hook. No matter how well we think we're doing, we are all human and capable of slipping now and then. And that's when awareness that we are being an ass is important. A lot of times we try to justify *why* we are being a jerk, but more often than not there is no justification. Honesty means checking your own beliefs and justifications.

Life is hard. Golf is hard. Being a jerk is easy, especially when life and golf keep testing our patience. Here are several questions that I will follow with a simple answer: Should he have refrained from hurling his club at the local wildlife? Yes. Was it wise to insult his friend's wife. No. Did the universe say it was alright to scream at another golfer? No. Should she cheat on her scorecard? No. Will she improve the other driver's day if she gives him the finger? No. In life and in golf, the most important guiding principle is simple. It can get you out of most any situation and it's only four simple words: "Don't be a jerk." Please. Really. No, this isn't one of those times, and that's not an excuse. Don't do it. Stop. Don't be a jerk. With all of the craziness going on in the world these days it is more important than ever that each and every one of us commit to setting a good example.

One time I was playing a round at a nice course outside of Portland, OR with a really good college friend of mine. Mind you, we were 15 years out of college and we had both grown a lot, but he was still living up to his college nickname of 'anger management.' I think it was the 11th hole where he hit a terrible shot and just absolutely lost his ever loving mind. He started spinning around and whipping his iron through the air. It sailed directly over my head and came within feet of decapitating me. I think my response was 'what the f#@k dude?!', which loosely translates to, 'lose your temper and be a child if you want, but don't drag me into this. You almost killed me!'

Our tantrums can have serious effects on others around us and that is not acceptable. Anger is a path to nowhere. Yet so many of us repeatedly choose this path. We are constantly losing our temper with people who differ from us. We are obsessed with being right, as opposed to doing what is right, and we feel that we have to defend our opinions as if they are the most important things in the world. I hope we haven't lost the ability to accept each other's differences; that we can still relate to each other based on our similarities. To me it's simple. I don't care about anyone's religious beliefs, political beliefs, sexual preference, socioeconomic status, or skin color. What I care about is whether or not they are a jerk. We have to learn to treat each other with respect.

If we truly desire to create a better world for our future generations then we must all take responsibility to do our best. We can't teach kids how to act unless we learn ourselves. The days of "do as I say and not as I do" are long gone, and for good reason. Young people are much smarter and more aware today than we give them credit for. In the words of the great athlete and human being Bill Russell, "I have a motto. There is no such thing as other people's children in America. That's the next generation of Americans." We are all responsible.

If America had a national jerk meter, we'd be in the red. Generally speaking, we're not doing a great job. I could provide an array of factual statistics to support this claim, but it wouldn't be as much fun as reading this anecdote. A few years ago a good friend and I got paired up with one of those awful, criticizing "Caddie Daddies," who was instructing his 10-year-old son on the golf course. This kid had a very natural swing, was probably considered gifted for his age, and seemed like a sweet kid, despite the misdirected parenting he was getting. The dad was constantly badgering and belittling the boy instead of encouraging him. The father's focus was targeted on what his son was doing wrong and almost never on what he did right. It all finally came to a head when on the 14th green, the dad practically stomped his feet and screamed like a child "You have no patience!!" How can we teach a child to have patience if we have none? Obviously we can't.

How can we expect kids to act with poise and grace if we're running around, stomping our feet and throwing tantrums? I see way too many 'adults' on and off the golf course losing their temper and acting like babies. Golf is the perfect antidote to stem the tide of Hurricane Jerk-face. Golf is mentally and emotionally challenging. That's why programs like

The First Tee are so important, because they provide leadership and teach us how to use the game as a teaching tool. The lesson? Don't be a jerk. We need more of these programs and each and every one of us needs to do our part to set the best example we can.

The great existentialist philosopher Jean-Paul Satre once said that 'we should treat every decision and every action as if all of humanity was at stake.' His suggestion was that before we do or say anything we should ask ourselves, "what if everyone acted like that?" I agree whole-heartedly.

We should use golf as a tool to work on our temper and as a place to practice staying calm and kind while experiencing adversity. Each one of us needs to take responsibility for our actions and set an example of how to deal with our emotions as if all humanity depended on it, because on some level it does. Let's commit to supporting one another, so it will be just a little easier to be kind to ourselves and everyone else. Golf is a great place to practice being kind. It is a place where we can practice doing things for others. Pick up an opponent's club and hand it to them or buy them a beer at the turn. The more we do things for others the better we feel, so practice often.

How are you doing with keeping your temper under control on or off of the golf course? When's the last time you acted like a jerk? What example are you setting for others?

Score	Explanation	Example
Eagle	Buddha? Is that you?	You got ice water for the racist guy after he got heat exhaustion at the hate rally.
Birdie	You are usually kind regardless of what's happening.	You broke up the fight between a liberal and a conservative and reminded them they have the same mother.
Par	Sometimes kind. Sometimes not.	You gave dirty look to slow old lady at the market check out line. Helped her pick up the grocery bag she dropped in the parking lot.
Bogey	You're kind of a jerk most of the time.	You yelled at the girl scout because Samoas are dangerous given your coconut allergy!
Double Bogey	Your friends would describe you as a 'raging a-hole'.	You smashed your neighbor's brake lights because she encroached into your parking space by 6 inches.

Score _____

Pro Tip

Reminding yourself what you are committed to in life is a really important and worthy thing to keep in mind. When you lose your temper, take a step back and ask yourself if this tantrum is worth it. Oftentimes, not only is it not worth it, but it's also keeping you from what you really want – enjoyment on the golf course, a loving relationship with your partner, etc.

Practice Drills

♦ *Double Bogey* ♦ Anger management therapy can be a good option for those who have severe issue controlling their temper. Seek out a therapist or a local support group so you can talk to someone before things really get out of hand.

♦ *Bogey* ♦ Call a time out. Time outs are not just for kids. They can be very effective for adults as well, especially when we are acting like children. The next time you start to blow up, remove yourself from the situation and go to a quiet place by yourself for a few minutes so you can calm down. On the golf course you can do this by taking a bathroom break or a stroll through the woods along the fairway.

♦ *Par* ♦ Sign up to be a mentor with Big Brothers, Big Sisters or some other mentoring program. Not only is it a great thing to provide guidance to a child who needs it, but it also makes us accountable for setting a positive example for others.

Hole 13

Integri-tee

"Golf is a game of ego, but it is also a game of integrity: the most important thing is you do what is right when no one is looking."
— Tom Watson

One thing that The First Tee does well is to teach children the value of integrity. The program also fosters growth in the areas of honesty, sportsmanship, respect, responsibility and courtesy. It could be said that most of their core values are necessary components of integrity. Our children learn integrity when they see us living with it. The golf course is a great place to develop and practice this skill, which will serve us well in other areas of our lives.

Many of us know the simple definition of integrity to be 'the quality of being honest and having strong moral principles.' But integrity as defined by Wikipedia is a 'concept of consistency of actions, values, methods, measures, principles, expectations and outcomes.' Integrity and golf both require consistency. We don't get to choose when to live with integrity. Integrity isn't something we achieve or gain. We can never perfect our mastery of integrity. It's more like a beacon, a way to orient our lives. We are either living with or near integrity, or straying from it. It's something that we either commit to working on, or we don't.

Golf has forced me to measure my own sense of integrity. It is the only sport where the participants regulate themselves, which makes integrity absolutely crucial. To play well and be respected, a player's word must be impeccable. Such is the same with life, yet it seems that so many of us are incredibly cavalier with our words. I'm not saying that good golfers and good people haven't stretched the truth at times. What I AM saying is that we never 'get away' with anything. We always know whether we are close to or far from integrity, whether we'll admit this or not. In that regard, we can convince ourselves of whatever we want, but ultimately, deep down, we know the truth. One thing about the truth is that you can run, but you can't hide.

This is why it is important to be careful and thoughtful with our words. It is human to make mistakes and slip-up. A person of integrity is not perfect, but he will immediately cop to the mistake. Admitting when we've faltered is a big deal and it can instantaneously restore our integrity. The thing is that our word has incredible power to be used for good...or not so good. We can really and truly lift someone's spirits by saying the right thing at the right time. Conversely, we can throw figurative daggers at them with biting words that can sting or leave permanent emotional marks. If we're trying to be the best version of ourselves at all times, shouldn't we choose to use our words to raise ourselves and others up, as opposed to breaking each other down?

Never mind golf for a moment. This is some of the best life advice I have ever received. Words have power. One of the things that makes me cringe the most in life is how loosely and casually people throw around the word 'hate.' Hate is a word with immense power. As a friend of mine always says, "Hitler you hate, anything else is just something you don't like." I think that sums it up well. Save a word like "hate" for when it is needed. But I digress. The point is that words have power and so does 'our word'. When we give our word to somebody it has power to be positive if we keep it or negative if we don't. We all remember the children's story about the boy who cried wolf falsely so many times that when the wolf really came, no one listened... and he got eaten.

In golf there is an agreed upon set of rules. Whether or not we collectively choose to change them slightly or not for our Saturday morning match is fairly irrelevant. What is important is that once agreed upon, we play by the rules that were set forth. Either we will have a reputation as someone who can be trusted or we will fall short and develop a negative reputation. People carry reputations around like luggage. We want ours to be light and easy to explain. The stickers on our luggage should tell people that we can be relied upon; let's make conscious choices and think critically about how our actions could influence our reputation and our relationship with integrity.

In 2010, English born Brian Davis found himself in a play-off against Jim Furyk at the Heritage golf tournament on Hilton Head Island, SC. Davis had won twice on the European Tour and was in search of his first PGA Tour win. This was a huge moment for him and it all came to a screeching halt when he called a two-stroke penalty on himself and thereby sealed his own 2nd place fate.

Davis' approach shot had missed the green. His ball came to rest in a marked hazard among some twigs, reeds, and grass. Rule 13.4 of golf prohibits a golfer to 'touch or move a loose impediment lying in or touching the hazard.' As Davis began his swing he barely touched a loose reed upon takeaway, which was a violation of this rule. No one else saw it. It did not influence the outcome of the shot. Yet he knew he had done it and called the penalty. Both his playing opponent and the tour rules official asked him if he was absolutely sure he had done this. His response was, "I know I did." Fair or not, he had broken an agreed upon rule and had to suffer the consequences. Davis later stated that 'I could not have lived with myself if I had not (called the infraction).' He had lost the chance to win – and he had gained enormous respect from his peers and from fans around the world.

We all make mistakes. When we do it's important to forgive ourselves for not being perfect. Then we must admit that we slipped up and accept the consequences related to our actions.

Whether we think the consequences are fair is irrelevant. Golf is not always fair, which is yet another reason why it is such a great teacher of life. If we play with great integrity it becomes even more challenging and the payoff is even greater.

Another example of integrity is found at the bottom of a divot. Like that one that was made at the end of the day as the group was rushing to stay ahead of the incoming thunderstorm. One might say 'what does it matter if I replace every divot or repair every ball mark?' It matters to the woman playing by the letter of the law against her friends who's drive just settled into an empty divot. It matters to the guy who is trying to make a putt to win a match but now has to putt through a minefield to do so. We are all on this planet together. Let's treat each other the way we would like to be treated. To put another way, if we don't want to have to hit out of an empty divot, let's commit to ALWAYS replacing the ones we make. Let's shake on it right now. Okay?

We can all use golf as a training ground to learn to live our lives with integrity. This is no easy task. It's hard to 'call penalties' on ourselves when we've made a mistake. It takes great strength to face our own imperfections, and do what is required to restore integrity. And it's very important to take on this challenge. As we practice integrity on and off the golf course, that example spreads and things improve over time. Each of us has a role to play in creating a world filled with integrity and it starts with each of us policing ourselves the best we can. Then it is up to the next generation to choose whether to follow the path we have blazed.

Are you living a life of integrity? Did you recently forget to replace a divot? Are there mistakes you'd like to own and take responsibility for? Can people take you for your word – or do they let your words go in one ear and out the other knowing that they don't mean anything?

Score	Explanation	Example
Eagle	Abe Lincoln would endorse your integrity.	Told your wife you lied to her. You didn't skip family dinner due to work but because you're taking art classes so you can paint her a portrait of her parents for her birthday.
Birdie	You are very honest but not perfect.	You told the cashier they forgot to ring up the case of bottled water. Who would care about the candy you ate in the bulk section?
Par	Integrity? If I feel like it.	You reminded your cousin that you owe him $200 from last weekend when he blacked out but kept those photos in case you needed a favor one day.
Bogey	You are not quite the most straight shooter.	Watched your neighbor's cat for a week and only fed her twice. It's not like she can tell on you.
Double Bogey	You could make a used car salesman blush.	Told your mom you were busy with work and couldn't help her so you could go to 50-cent wing night at Hooters.

Score _____

Pro Tip

There's no such thing as 'little white lies'. You are either a truthful person or you are not. Every time you say something, it counts in the positive or negative column of the type of person you are. Bring your awareness to the things you say to yourself and others and make note of when you are not being truthful. Even the small mistruths matter because it's a slippery slope from small lies to big ones. Remain aware of how often you are living a life out of integrity and begin to restore that integrity by creating a new narrative based on always being truthful with yourself and everyone else.

Practice Drills

• *Double Bogey* ◆ Call a penalty on yourself this week. Pick something small to start. Tell a coworker you ate their leftovers from the communal fridge. Tell your mom you took $10 from her wallet without asking. Tell your girlfriend that you lied about studying so you could go out with the boys. Baby steps are important so we can build towards a life of integrity.

• *Bogey* ◆ Make a list of all of the areas in your life where you are out of integrity. There could be some big ones, and for most there will be lots of small ones. Write them down, and then next to each one, identify a basic change that you can make based on integrity being a priority.

• *Par* ◆ No more Mulligans! Stop giving yourself do-over privileges. We have to learn to live with our mistakes. The best way to do that is by not trying to erase them but by moving forward regardless of how we have messed up. Don't allow yourself to hit another tee shot, restart that video game or jump from relationship to relationship without ever facing your faults that need improvement.

Hole 14

Inclusivi-tee

"In the end it's still a game of golf, and if, at the end of the day, you can't shake hands with your opponents and still be friends, then you've missed the point."
— Payne Stewart

There is a fairly common misconception that the word GOLF is derived from an acronym for "Gentlemen Only Ladies Forbidden." This has been proven to be false. It actually originates from an old Scottish/Dutch word meaning 'club' or 'to strike.' Although, given the long history of private golf clubs excluding people based on gender or race, it is no wonder that the fallacy has become recognized as truth. We live in a complex era where the truth can be called 'fake news,' and 'fake news' can be seen as truth. Thankfully as the world evolves, so does the game of golf and the view of many private golf clubs. It was years before Augusta National Golf Club - that storied club known as much for The Masters tournament and its pristine landscaping as it was for being an old, rich white man's club - admitted black members. We've now seen the club accept a black woman, former secretary of state Condoleezza Rice, as a member. Augusta also recently announced plans to host the National Women's Amateur Championship. Indeed, the tide has turned and the age of inclusivity is upon us.

Because of its checkered past on the subject, the game of golf finds itself with a unique opportunity to claim a leadership role with regard to inclusivity. As a culture and as a game, the community of golf must continue to move toward a place where no one is wrongfully excluded solely based on gender, ethnicity, sexual preference, religion, socio-economic status or any other perceived barrier that causes division, rather than inclusion.

Think about the Tiger Woods effect on the game. Where would the game be right now without Tiger's influence? Because Tiger was such a special athlete and golfer, he helped break down the racial barriers that once clouded this great game. Because he was so good, and made so much money for everyone, the game had to reconsider its racist past and find a way out of it. Thankfully for all of us, it did just that and in the process opened the floodgates of amazing athletes of all ethnicities pouring into the professional game. Many of these athletes might have played other sports if it weren't for Tiger. It also showed amateurs all over the world that no matter what their ethnic background, gender, or political view, there was a place for them in the game of golf if they wanted it.

Diversity has changed the game of golf permanently for the better. This is a great microcosmic example for humanity. "United we stand; divided we fall", is not just a mantra for a country but for an entire species. In times of tragedy it's easy for us to look past the imaginary barriers we've created in our world. When there is a natural disaster or terrorist attack, we don't stop to ask someone's race, sexual preference or voting history before helping them. We just do it because it's the right thing to do. If we do that more often than just in times of strife, the world will be a better place and the game of golf a better game.

Here's funny story about inclusivity and breaking down archaic barriers. One year a couple of buddies and I went to Tiger's World Golf Challenge tournament at Sherwood Country Club in Westlake, CA. For those who are not familiar, Sherwood is one of the most expensive and most exclusive country clubs in America; it is steeped in tradition. In fact, at the time of our visit, the weekend of the tournament was the only time that women were allowed in the members' bar of the clubhouse.

The night before we went to the tournament, our group was excited to catch-up and so we had a late night in Hollywood. The next morning I just threw on a hooded sweatshirt and headed out the door to the tournament – not expecting anything more than to be walking the grounds with our general admission passes. I had invited a girl that I was dating to tag along with us. It turned out that she knew the caddie for Anthony Kim, who was playing that year. Next thing you know we're being invited into the player's lounge (otherwise known as the member's bar), with access to full buffet and open bar.

Only minutes later we were doing shots with Padraig Harrington's buddies from Ireland, and having a grand old time. And there I was, a brownish guy in a hoodie with no undershirt. Talk about breaking down traditional barriers! The afternoon continued and before long we were whooping it up and laughing our faces off. Sure, we got some funny looks (which we ignored), and we also had several conversations with staff members there, which were no doubt a nice way to vet us and make sure we weren't party crashers. Really the staff could not have been more kind, and most of them ended up sharing a few laughs with us before going back to work. We stayed all day and were the last ones to leave. It was probably mere moments before we would have finally worn out our welcome. A good time was had by all and the member's bar at Sherwood was indeed brightened that day.

Scientists have proven that scientific experiments are inherently improved in a diverse group as opposed to a non-diverse group. The reasoning being simply that those in the group who are similar will have similar outlooks on how to solve a problem where the group filled with more diversity will have a more varied outlook on problem-solving, thus offering more potential solutions and having a better chance of finding the best one.

One could say that these same benefits come to the game of golf through diversity. The drastic globalization of the game just in the last few years has led to a new crop of players from Asia, Indonesia, South America and Central America. Think about the potential long-term positive effect this could have on the game of golf. It's more than a surface concern, this means a wider array of opinions and viewpoints to help grow the game. Imagine a foursome with someone from the slums of Mumbai playing alongside an aristocrat from England, a farmer's daughter from Chile, and a businessman from South Africa. One might say, 'they have nothing on common. Why would they play together?' Umm hello – they all play golf! That seems like a great, shared interest from which to build a friendship. Golf can be the Petri dish where the world experiments in turning away from its former divisive nature and moves towards a place where inclusion and diversity are not only accepted but also celebrated.

There are those who would resist change and progress, longing for the days when a foursome all looked and thought the same. But golf is not just a rich, white man's game anymore, and that is a very good thing.

It is so silly that in 2018, we still see each other as separate entities that we must compete against. We're like toddlers on the playground with views like 'my town is better than yours, my country is better than yours, my race is better than yours, my golf game is better than yours – nah nah nah nah nah nah'. Who cares?! We make each other better through collaboration and mutual encouragement much more than we do through competition. To be clear, I think that 'everyone gets a trophy' culture is absurd and am in no way condoning that. Competition can still be a great learning tool, as long as it's prioritized appropriately.

Look no further than the young generation of superstar professional golfers like Rickie Fowler, Jordan Spieth and Justin Thomas. These guys go on vacations and travel together when not competing, and yet they still want to win when the next tournament starts. As much as one might cheer for another once he is no longer in contention, they still never want to lose against their friends because they know they'll never hear the end of it. But they always compete with good sportsmanship, ever remembering that their friendships outside the ropes will always be much more valuable than any trophy that they can win.

It's hearing about relationships like this that give me hope about the millennial generation. Our culture likes to focus on their shortcomings. We talk about this generation being entitled and literally like saying "literally" all of the time. Every generation has shortcomings when they are young. As elders, it's our job to attempt to help them move past immature habits while finding and fostering positive attributes. One of the great glimmers of hope of this young generation is that, in general, they don't see the previously accepted divisions of race, gender, socio economic status, etc. They innately see a world where inclusivity is a birth right – as long as you're not a hate-filled jerk. (There it is again. Don't be a jerk.)

Most people agree that the current status of our society is grim, but many disagree on why. I think it's wise to look at it from the point of view that there is no 'us and them.' There is only us and we have to find a way forward. Perhaps it's time we started letting golf lead the way? If the old 'rich white man's game' can find a path towards inclusivity then maybe there is hope for humanity after all.

Are you doing all you can to create space for inclusivity? Or are you mired in archaic, divisive views?

Score	Explanation	Example
Eagle	Inclusivity is second nature to you.	Your dinner parties are known to be more diverse than the U.N.
Birdie	You're generally welcoming.	You regularly volunteer at the LGBT center.
Par	You are not sure whether inclusivity works.	You think MLK's views on equality were B.S. because he cheated on his wife. Wait, what?
Bogey	Is inclusivity really necessary?	Do we really need to include those kids from the other side of the tracks in our middle class little league?
Double Bogey	Exclusivity a good thing.	People should stay put in the countries where they are born.

Score _____

Pro Tip

Work to get out of your comfort zone and interact with people who are different from you. You could join a social club with a diverse base or a multicultural golf league. The biggest thing is to find things that will help you get past your pre-conceived notions about people so you can eventually judge everyone by the content of their character and nothing else.

Practice Drills

* *Double Bogey* * Throw yourself into situations where you have to interact with other people who are different from you. Go to a golf course you've never been to as a single and get paired up with 3 other random people. Go to a social event that is out of your comfort zone and see who you connect with.

* *Bogey* * Join a co-ed athletic league. Whether it's golf, soft-ball or kick ball, we can learn a lot about inclusivity from having regular contact where we are pulling for each other to do our best.

* *Par* * Volunteer at a local soup kitchen or children's hospital. Not only does this help other people who need it, but it also helps us remember that we are all human and ultimately all the same despite our different circumstances. As an added benefit, there is no better feeling in the world than sharing a small act of kindness with someone who feels inferior in some way.

Hole 15

Not So
Great Expectations

"Peace begins when expectations end."
— *Sri Chinmoy*

When I woke up that morning, I had expected to have more time to shower and get ready. Not having this time made me feel unsure of myself. During the drive to the course, I ran into a ton of traffic and all I could think about was how much golf time I as losing as I sat there stuck in my car. I needed to get into the locker room so I could change into my lucky shirt. I needed a couple minutes to buy water to drink on the course. I needed my partner to be ready and waiting at the first tee. I needed, I needed, I needed… and none of it made me happy.

Learning to manage expectations can have positive influence on our lives. We've all heard time and time again how expectations ultimately lead to frustration. Yet so many of us continue to go blindly through life inextricably tied to rigid expectations that were unconsciously set by us. So how do we learn to get some control in the matter? Like everything else it starts with awareness, continues with commitment, and ends with acceptance.

Now some of you might be thinking, 'Wait a minute, Z. On the 5th hole you told us to visualize how we want things to be. If we are visualizing aren't we setting expectations?' Not necessarily - and certainly not ideally. You may also recall that on the 6th hole we discussed visualizing, then committing to the moment of impact, and ultimately releasing attachment to the outcome. Releasing attachment to outcome is just a fancy way to say, 'letting go of expectations.'

Basically the concept is that we should imagine a picture in our head of what we want, stay present at all times and focus on current moment. The truth is there is only so much we can control and then a whole bunch of other stuff that we cannot control. It's in trying to exert control over the things that are out of our control where our expectations grab hold of us and drag us down into the divots of disappointment.

It's easy to get caught up in the cycle of accomplishment. A process that calls for us to be proactive and 'take control of our life.' A cycle that causes us to forget that there are things well beyond our control. Before long we are working late into the night on that important proposal, or calling too often because we're focused on the end result. Rather than enjoy the beginnings of the relationship, we want the result, the commitment and the status. I'm not saying, we should go to bed early and forget the proposal. I'm also not saying we shouldn't call someone we feel attracted to; what I'm saying is it's good to know when to let it be.

Tomorrow is not promised to any of us. We are all subject to the potential freak accident, a terrorist attack, pianos falling from the sky. If one of those things happens, then it changes the way we view the things that we typically focus on (like the proposal or relationship). It is important to fully embrace the moments that we are gifted. Trying to control outcomes can compromise our quality of life.

I'll never forget the first time I played Torrey Pines in La Jolla, CA. I had seen this gorgeous course on TV so many times and now here I was! I'd been hitting the ball well, and my game was strong. I was brimming with confidence and had an expectation of playing well on this spectacular course. But that was the wrong expectation. Instead, I should have just focused on enjoying myself. Not only did I play terribly, I didn't have much fun either. My only focus was on how I was playing below my perceived capabilities. My expectations literally ruined a day that I had looked forward to for many years.

So if we are not in control then why even bother? Does it even matter? Yes! The idea is that we bother with the things that we can and should control. We also identify the things we can't or shouldn't control. Once we do that, it's time to stop and watch with wonder as life beautifully unfolds in front of our eyes. It's time to watch with no emotional attachment whatsoever, to forget about results and just admire the flight of our lives.

Standing on the tee box of the 190-yard downhill par 3 at Butterbrook Golf Course in Stow, MA, I remember gazing a the leaves on a fall day. It was 2015, and I had decided to refocus my expectations in a round that was not going well. I had been paired with a couple of young guys that were not very good and were playing considerably below there own modest standards. In fact, they thought it necessary to take that moment to apologize to me for playing so poorly saying, "We promise we're not this bad" as they bought some beers to try to relax.

I stuck my tee in the ground. "Guys, there's no need to apologize. I'm playing like crap, too. I'm just trying to focus on hitting good shots." Taking my own advice, I settled myself, visualized the shot I wanted to hit, committed to the moment of impact and let go of any expectations of where the ball would go. I made a great swing, striking the ball purely. I looked up and the flight and spin of the ball were exactly what I had envisioned with a slightly lower trajectory that I had hoped. The ball landed about 10 yards in front of the green. Topspin caused it to take a sweet bounce toward hole. As it rolled along the green it seemed to be tracking right at the flag as I said 'hit the pin.' And it did hit the pin – and fell right into the hole. This is still the only hole-in-one I have ever hit. And it never would have happened had I not reworked my expectations in the moments leading up to my swing.

Life and golf are supposed be fun and I've noticed that I have a lot more joy with both if I don't kid myself by pretending that I'm always in control. I need to constantly remind myself to take a truthful look at the things that are within my sphere of influence. Only then can I clearly identify those things that are beyond my ability to control. Managing expectations is the first step to letting go. Detach from the need to force a specific result. Remember to visualize, commit to the moment of impact, and then release attachment to outcome.

How are you doing with regard to managing expectations and giving up control? Are unrealized expectations causing you painful disappointment?

Score	Explanation	Example
Eagle	You have preferences but no expectations.	You thought you were going to get that promotion. Oh well now you can coach your son's soccer team.
Birdie	For the most part you keep expectations at bay but...	It still pisses you off that your teenagers won't clean their own dishes.
Par	Unmet expectations bother you but you move quickly past them.	I can't believe Hunan Palace is closed on Weds nights! I really wanted egg rolls. Let's try the new Greek place.
Bogey	Unrealized expectations still bum you out.	You remained mad for days after your sister beat you at Scrabble – which was only because she got the good letters
Double Bogey	Expectations run your life, and make you miserable.	You thought this would be the year that your dead-beat boyfriend would finally propose after 10 years.

Score _____

Pro Tip

Use expectation management on the golf course to help you do the same in other areas of your life. Consider making your pre shot routine 1. Clear your mind 2. Visualize the shot 3. Commit to the moment of impact and then 4. Release all attachment to outcome – as it is now out of your control from there. The goal is to refocus on that which you can and should control and let go of that which you cannot. This will serve you on the golf course. You just might get that elusive hole-in-one. More importantly, it will serve you in all other areas of your life.

Practice Drills

• *Double Bogey* • Let your spouse, partner or friend plan a night out for you. You don't get any say in where you go, what you eat, how long it lasts. This is a great way to learn to let go of trying to control outcomes. Your only expectation should be to enjoy it no matter what happens.

• *Bogey* • Do something that is intimidating to you. Write a poem; paint a picture or do something else that is out of your comfort zone. Visualize how you would like it to come out, do the best you can at the task, then DO NOT judge the outcome at all one way or the other. Just let it be what it is.

• *Par* • If you really want to challenge yourself, why not join an improvisational troop? I can't think of a better place to practice releasing attachment to outcome, as you literally never know what is going to be said or happen next.

Hole 16

Critic's Choice

*"Mistakes are a part of the game. It's how well
you recover from them, that's the mark of a great player."*
— Alice Cooper

One thing that I've found to be a universal truth in life is that for each of us there is no harsher critic than the voice inside our own heads. So many of us expect some sort of self-perfection and then are disappointed when it is not attained. This quality becomes very evident when playing golf below our standards. I've called myself unspeakable names. Really, I should probably take myself to couples therapy. It's even worse when I miss what should be an easy shot. I should give myself a break, and be more forgiving of my own perceived imperfections, but man that's a hard one.

We are human beings. We are not perfect and we are not meant to be. This is why golf is such a great metaphor for life. There is no such thing as a perfect golfer. We all have good days and bad days. We all hit good and bad shots, relative to our skill level. That's just the way it is. This is a reflection of our humanity.

We will always make mistakes and when we do we must forgive ourselves, learn the lesson at hand and then move on looking for an opportunity to do our best next time. We are the only ones who see every flaw that we have. Everyone else is so consumed with their own shortcomings that they rarely, if ever, are as critical in their views. Not that it matters what other people think about any of us. In fact the best piece of advice I ever received was, 'It's none of your business what other people think of you.' It's not that other opinions don't matter. The point is that it's literally none of my business. Remember this when fears about other's judgments become overwhelming. It's their business and ultimately shaped by their own self-perception. People will project what they want. What I think of myself is what's important. That is that part that can be controlled.

It's also important to note here that our judgments of others are just a reflection of our own critical self-perception. So whether it's figuratively beating ourselves up or criticizing someone else over a perceived flaw, the way to calm and heal is to look inward, take off the Judge's robe, and give ourselves and everyone else a well-deserved pardon.

Author Sanaya Roman said, "having inner peace means committing to letting go of self-criticism and self-doubt." I'm sure we can all agree that life and golf are enjoyed at optimal levels when we are at a place of inner peace. When a deep calm is present we are able to stroll through life (or a round of golf) with a playful outlook that allows us the freedom to take what comes in stride.

Personally I'm not a huge fan of playing golf matches, although I do enjoy them on occasion. For me one of the greatest things about the game of golf is that it's really about playing against yourself. Every shot is an opportunity to overcome the limits that we suspect we might have. Or as Sam Snead put it, 'Forget your opponents. Always play against par.' Off of the course I play my life against an envisioned par, an imagined standard that keeps me focused on good works. This helps me avoid the toxicity of competition and comparison.

That's the thing with golf and life. We fool ourselves into thinking we are playing against others, but really all we are doing is striving to be the best we can be on any given day. We cannot be at our best when we are being overly critical with ourselves. It's good to know what we're capable of and to want to strive to do our best. Yet when it doesn't go the way we hoped, we have to have self-empathy in order to move on to the next challenge.

Golf provides a great opportunity for self-reflection. Every golfer misses shots. Even the best golfers in the world miss shots. I tell myself this when I miss a shot. The really great ones are able to accept their mistakes and move forward while staying present and in the moment. Everyone who has ever played the game of golf has lost their composure and cussed themselves out. But how often has that brutally harsh negative self-talk actually lead to an improvement during the round that is being played? Almost never.

Losing patience with myself and hammering home feelings of low self-worth is generally not going to help me accomplish my goals and it will certainly not help me enjoy the journey as I try to be the best person I'm capable of being.

Let's look at Sergio Garcia's path to his first major championship. Here's a guy that burst onto the scene, and reminded many of his idol Seve Ballesteros. Unlike Seve, Sergio didn't garner a convincing major win early in his career. A win that would perhaps prove (if only to himself) that he was good enough to belong among the elite on tour. Although I wonder if things would have been different had he beaten Tiger in the PGA Championship when he was 19. For the next 17 years, he would be one of the best golfers in the world, winning 30 times and having several near misses at what became an increasingly elusive major tournament victory. Many wrote off his chances to win the next major, and even Sergio himself said 'I'm not good enough...I don't have the thing I need to have,' after another emotional loss at the 2012 Masters. I almost fell over when I heard that. This guy is one of the elite of the elite and he was questioning whether he was good enough to win when it counted most. How was this possible? I had forgotten that Sergio, although and elite talent and blessed with rare gifts, was also just like the rest of us. He was his own worst critic.

Luckily his journey had a happy ending. Just 5 years later in 2017, Sergio finally broke through at the Masters, where he won what is often considered the most prestigious of all majors. If you watched that tournament, you may remember that there was something seemingly different about Sergio that weekend. He had a strange calm about him. He was always laughing and having fun, and he often had a look in his eyes that seemed to say he knew it was his time. It was likely no coincidence that this happened after he got engaged. The major life change seemed to suit him. It was likely no coincidence that the day he won was Seve's birthday. And it was certainly no coincidence that he finally hoisted the trophy after 47 major starts, when he mercifully removed the self-doubting thoughts from his head and created space for belief in himself and the possibility of success.

I can give you another example of a more personal nature. Up until now I have never written anything more than a few blog posts, which in itself was only very recent. I never really gave any thought to the fact that I might be a writer of any kind. But a few years ago I started writing about things that I thought could help people and after a few blog posts and some really good feedback, I realized there was a chance I could develop as a writer. At that point I knew I had to write a book. What the heck would I write about? I'm not a writer. I don't know how to write a book. Even as I sit here typing this self-doubting thoughts continue to creep in. I wonder if it will make a shred of difference to a friend who is a golfer or a family member who is going through a tough time or to a stranger who just needed some perspective.

There were a million reasons to not write this book. And yet there I was typing away, and the challenge was similar to mastering golf. I had to focus on the present moment, believe in myself, and let go of any anxiety I might have about the result. Instead of pushing out worries about where the golf ball might land, I was now selectively ignoring the self-criticism that would likely try to explain the many ways I'm not good enough to be a writer. Instead, I realized that my job was to write the best book that I could. I had to let go of harsh self-criticism. It's up to the reader to decide if it is helpful. The reaction to this book is not my business.

One thing that occurred to me as I was writing the above is that this concept is true about any of us. The truth is most of us don't really know what we're doing the majority of the time. Even the most confident, egotistical politician really has very little clue what they are doing until it is done. That's not a judgment. That's just how life works. We're all going through moments and days (hopefully) doing the best we can and figuring it out as we go. If you need a further example just ask a parent of a one-day-old first child how confident they feel about their parenting skills. They have no clue how to be a parent – until they do it – and 99% of the time they figure it out along the way to become the best parent they are capable of being at that time. That's an extreme example of what we all experience all the time – especially when we endeavor into unchartered areas, which is where the greatest growth occurs. As Martin Luther King Jr. so eloquently put it, "Faith is taking the first step when you can't see the whole staircase."

Having faith in ourselves is crucial to everything that we endeavor to do. We don't need to know where we're going or how we'll get there. We don't need to know how we're going to get this ball from the trees and eventually in the hole. We just need to know that we can. This will not only improve our golf game but it can be a key component of building a society that so many claim to desire. If we all commit to focusing on reducing our own self-criticisms, we organically criticize one another a lot less. Harmonious individuals lead to harmonious towns, states, countries and planets.

At time of writing, I'm a solid double bogey on this hole – but working on it. What is your self-criticism score?

Score	Explanation	Example
Eagle	You are always kind to yourself.	You hysterically laugh at your silly absent-mindedness because you locked your keys in the car, again.
Birdie	You are usually accepting of your faults.	So what if you can't fix cars? That's why you are a AAA member.
Par	You struggle with self-acceptance but try to find the bright side.	You dislike how socially awkward you are. But then again you wouldn't have met Claire at the support group if you weren't.
Bogey	You are unnecessarily harsh on yourself	If you weren't so dumb you would have gotten that final Jeopardy clue and beat your son.
Double Bogey	You are brutally hard on yourself for trivial things.	You smash the remote while swearing at yourself because you forgot to record Matlock for your grandmother.

Score _____

Pro Tip

Give yourself a break!! You are not perfect and you are not meant to be. Your job is to do the best you can with what you have while learning not to judge yourself so harshly. It always helps me to remind myself that I'm not the only one judging myself so harshly. Literally everyone else is doing the same to himself or herself –consciously or subconsciously - whether they admit it or not. This awareness generally gets me to realize how silly it is and stop my judgmental thought patterns. Your unwarranted self-criticism is ultimately only holding you back from being the best version or yourself – so cut it out!

Practice Drills

◆ *Double Bogey* ◆ Ask a loved one or close friend to write you a letter describing all of the things they love about you. For this purpose it should be only the positives! We already know too well the negatives that constantly swirl through our heads. This is an opportunity to hear, in a positive way, how you are viewed from an outside source. Often we are so caught up in our negative self view, that we forget what people enjoy about us. Keep this letter with you and read it you're being hard on yourself.

◆ *Bogey* ◆ Adopt a positive mantra to replace the negative thoughts when they come. Some examples could be: "mistakes are a gift that help me learn and grow"; "I don't need to be perfect. I just need to do my best"; or "I can choose a positive self-view." Try this for a couple of weeks. Every time that negative voice starts up in your head stop, breathe and replace it with something positive. You might be surprised by the difference it makes.

♦ *Par* ♦ Surround yourself with positive people. Many of us have come to think it's normal to have close friends and family who are incredibly negative. This can be programmed at a young age by parents or teachers. This is not normal and it's not good! Take a look at the people your surround yourself with and cut ties with those who are constantly negative. Having a positive circle of friends can make a huge difference.

Hole 17

Lesson...The Pain

*"Missing a short putt does not mean you have to
hit your next drive out of bounds."*
— Henry Cotton

Through the most pain comes the most growth. Most of us have heard this and most of us have experienced this. We don't get to choose what the lessons are, when they come or how they are delivered. But we do get to choose how to approach the lesson at hand. We can resist it, dislike it, feel sorry for ourselves, or we can accept it for what it is and get on with learning and growing.

As long as we are here and as long as we play golf there will be lessons to learn. It's just the way it is. Resistance is futile. On the 8th hole we touched on learning lessons whether we are grinding or thriving through life or a game of golf. The concept of always learning is worth visiting here. Golf and life are games that we never master. Rather they are games that are designed to allow for perpetual growth through constant challenge. The sooner we learn that, the sooner we can get ourselves prepared to adjust on the fly no matter what comes our way.

What I've also learned is that golf and life can trick us into believing that we 'have it figured out.' Brief moments of clarity where everything seems to fall into place, are often followed by new obstacles placed in our path. I can choose to be constantly frustrated by the new challenges or I can choose to accept that these vicissitudes will continue. Either way, the Universe and the Golf Gods are not affected by how I react. They will continue to test me whether I like it or not.

Let's look back on the incredible run that Tom Watson made in the 2009 Open Championship at Turnberry. Watson is widely regarded as one of the best professional links course players in history, having won 5 previous Opens.

Now, he was 59 years-old and not only in contention but in the lead on the final hole, needing only a par to become the oldest major championship winner in history (and by more than a decade). I can still vividly remember watching this tournament. It was set up to be the biggest single underdog story in the history of sports. I've never felt so compelled to pull for someone (or some team) than I did that weekend. Unfortunately, the storybook ending was not meant to be.

With Watson's approach shot on the final hole heading towards the pin, it looked like it was actually about to happen. And then the ball took a hard bounce and trickled off the green. I mean it was really the bad break of all bad golf breaks, given what was at stake. Unable the get the ball up and down for par, Watson was relegated to a playoff vs. Stewart Cink, which he eventually lost. I was crushed. I'm still a little bummed about it to this day. I cannot imagine how Tom Watson felt then, and how he must feel now. I mean here was one of the real good guys of golf about to make history by beating the best current golfers in the world, and at the game's most lauded championship. It was setting up to be a phenomenal story for the ages, only for it all to be cruelly trampled upon at the last minute.

Even after almost 6 decades on this earth - by all accounts as a really good person - and several worldwide professional wins including 8 major championships, the Universe and Golf Gods were not done teaching Tom Watson harsh lessons. It seemed so cruel. Yet although Watson was likely to never to get another chance to win a major, what he did have was a chance to reflect on a tough lesson and grow both as a person and a golfer. Although it may have been tough to swallow, the old saying of 'win or lose, don't lose the lesson,' rang out loud and clear. Only Tom Watson knows what those lessons were for him. I can tell you from my perspective that I was reminded of how life and sports don't always play out the way we want them to go. And this is what makes winning that much sweeter when it actually happens. Incidentally, Watson did recently get a small token of revenge by beating a field of young competitors at the 2018 Masters Par 3 Contest, a victory that saw him become the oldest to ever win at the age of 68.

It is our choice whether to hang our heads and let the test get the best of us, or to embrace the opportunity to overcome adversity. That is the moment of truth. The reaction that we choose often defines who we will be moving forward. A great golf case in point is what happened to Dustin Johnson at the 2010 PGA Championship, and more importantly how he chose to embrace it and carry on with his career.

We now know DJ as one of the top golfers in the world, but at that time he was an up-and-coming golfer who had won 3 times on the PGA Tour and was poised to break though to put himself in elite status. With a one-shot lead at the PGA Championship at Whistling Straights in Wisconsin, Johnson found his ball in a trampled down dirt area. He incorrectly assumed that it was a waste area rather than one of the 1,000 areas that were deemed bunkers by a local rule that week. Because of the misunderstanding, he grounded his club on the dirt and was told in the scorer's tent that he would not be playing in a playoff with a chance to win his first major. Instead he incurred a two-stroke penalty and was done for the tournament.

This incredible turn of events could have caused even the most mentally tough athlete to wallow in sorrow or explode with anger. He had unknowingly beaten himself. This was the kind of thing that could take months or years to get over. But Dustin chose to learn the lesson. He had to be more attentive to the rules and carry on with his solid play. He was rewarded for staying positive by winning the third Fed Ex Cup playoff event just a few weeks later. He has since won 13 more times, including the 2016 U.S. Open ascending to the #1 world golf ranking. Interestingly enough DJ again received a penalty during the final round. Although everyone but the USGA agreed that the penalty was incorrect and the way they handled it was even worse. Johnson was told in the middle of the round about the penalty, but because he had been through similar instances and emotions, he was able to keep his focus and win, despite the unfair and improper ruling.

We all have similar opportunities every time we are faced with adversity. Whether it is fair or not we can choose to use it as a springboard to become mentally and emotionally stronger. We are not always in control of outside forces that might make things difficult for us. Yet we are always in control of who we choose to be, no matter what is happening around us. It can be easy to blame external forces, but this renders us powerless to find the best path forward.

The truth isn't affected by our beliefs, but the consequences of our beliefs can negatively affect our journey if left unchecked. The truth, in this case, is that we will always be presented with the opportunity to learn and grow, throughout this lifetime. We can choose to believe that or not. Either way the lessons will continue to come.

Will you learn them, grow and move on, or will you resist and ensure that the same lessons keep coming back over and over?

Score	Explanation	Example
Eagle	You always learn the lesson.	Thank you baby Jesus for giving me golf to work on my patience!
Birdie	Usually you walk away having learned something new.	Didn't see that campaign loss coming. Next election you will double efforts on social media messaging.
Par	Sometimes you feel like a lesson. Sometimes you don't.	Sunday: I'm never drinking again Thursday: This week sucks. 3 martinis should help.
Bogey	You get glimpses of clarity in between the pain.	This insurance company is impossible! At least I didn't get hurt. But when will those idiots send my damn check?!
Double Bogey	You curse the gods for your 'bad luck.'	The world always screws me. How come I got fired again?! Stupid jerks! Grrrrrr!

Score _____

Pro Tip

Realize that no matter where you are in life that the lessons will continue to present you with the opportunity to learn and grow. You can resist those chances or embrace them. The choice is yours and will have a dramatic effect on your journey for better or worse depending on what you do in the face of challenges. I'm one who believes that the chance to grow should always be accepted. If you learn to see challenges as opportunities to bring your life or game to greater heights, you will do things that you might have once thought impossible.

Practice Drills

• *Double Bogey* • If you're one of those people that think the world and everyone in it is out to get you then you need a serious wake up call. It's time to rewrite your history. Make a list of all of the bad things that have happened to you. If there are too many, just hit the highlights. Next to each one write down who was responsible. Beside each one of those, write down how you chose to react. Now take a step back and realize that no matter what happened and who was responsible that you were the one who chose how to move forward (or not).

• *Bogey* • I know we just did mantras in the last chapter, but I think it works again here and is really important. When major challenges present themselves, stop yourself before you get all wound up and say, "I am the one responsible for my actions and choices no matter what happens around me." Start taking responsibility so you can learn from adversity and move on.

• *Par* • This is another good opportunity to do some volunteering. When we are caught up in lamenting our woes, one of the best ways to put things in perspective is to get out of your own head and go help others. In this case maybe a shelter for battered women or a children's hospital would be a good place to get some perspective and spread some joy to others, which will create joy for you.

Hole 18

Enjoy The Journey

"Keep your sense of humor. There's enough stress in the rest of your life not to let bad shots ruin a game you're supposed to enjoy."
— Amy Alcott

Sometimes it's hard to concentrate for an entire four-plus hours of a golf. But the last hole is just as important as all of the others, so it's important to keep our focus. In this case it's the key to the whole conversation. Life and golf are supposed to be fun. Often many of us take them way too seriously which leads to incredible amounts of frustration and pain. When I'm playing golf, I try to keep it simple, lighten up, and enjoy the wild ride. I've noticed that I make things so much harder on myself, harder than they need to be, when I think in ways that are heavy and serious.

Life and golf are a gift. Neither are going to go as I would like, but so what? They are both still amazing. So I'm here to declare that I intend to soak in every moment of beauty I can. I am going to drink every drink, shake every hand, and watch every shot as if it's the most important one will ever take. I accept the challenge to live on the simplest level, to sense my life as happening in a continuous series of moments - each one being the most important in the time that it occurs.

Happiness is not something driven by outside forces, but rather something that comes from within. We can strive to find material things or 'perfect' golf shots that provide fleeting moments of joy, but that is not true happiness. In EVERY moment we can choose happiness and joy. It can be said that of course there are severely dark moments when choosing happiness is not honest, and I understand this. What I'm talking about is not the day after an extreme tragedy, illness, or death. Sometimes we need time to mourn and heal. I'm talking about the rest of our lives. The other 98% of it. We can own that if we decide to choose the moment.

Golf has helped me to practice choosing a joyful state. I've had trouble and anxiety in my life, and I've experienced the feeling of being caught up in competing against others. I wouldn't wish these experiences on the reader but I suspect these feelings aren't totally foreign. Theodore Roosevelt once said that "comparison is the thief of joy," and he was right. Measuring myself against other people, or against other golfers often takes some of the joy and wonder out of the game. And this is all supposed to be fun!

A group of friends and I used to play the "Life is Good" golf tournament the day after Thanksgiving every year in Long Beach, CA. There were teams and prizes and money up for grabs – and make no mistake, we competed to beat each other. There were hilariously epic bouts of smack-talking every year. And yet every year at the end of the day, we sat together having drinks, reminiscing and talking about how lucky we were to be together and share the joys of the game. That was the whole point of the tournament, to take a step back and enjoy life with close friends. Win or lose, those are some of my best golf memories. No matter what happened, things were always kept in perspective and the ultimate goal was to have fun together.

As I was working on the edits and re-writes on this book one of the guys in that group passed away suddenly from a heart attack. Tom was a marginal golfer but a world-class smack-talker who could drink like a Russian vodka distiller. The thing was that his verbal jabs never came across as mean-spirited because Tom was, deep down, one of the kindest people I've ever known. Because of his jolly nature and his kind heart, we'll miss him terribly. That was the point of our yearly LIG tournament – to enjoy the gift of time. It will run out one day.

I'm not going to tell anyone else what to do. I'm telling you that I've made a choice. I'm going to enjoy the journey. I'm not going to complain about the bumps and inconveniences along the way. I know the power is in my hands and my heart. I'm going to get over it. I'm going to swing my swing, live in the moment of impact, and swing away. I'm going to let everyone into my club, forgive myself, see the opportunities and learn from the mistakes. I'm going to eat the soup when it's still hot and wink at the girl. This doesn't make me special. Anyone can make this choice.

One of my favorite golfers that is the perfect expression of joy on the golf course is Matt Kuchar. If you've ever watched him play you can't tell whether he just made eagle or double bogey. No matter what happens he always has that huge radiant smile on his face. Of course like any golfer or any human being he has frustrations and disappointments, but you never see him fundamentally change. He seemingly always chooses joy as his way of being which makes him really fun to watch.

I was once talking to my friend Jason Gore who was feeling really down about his game at the time. Here was a guy that had won a PGA tournament and was wondering whether he was up for this challenge anymore. The pressure under which these professionals play is crazy. But I told him, "Jay, don't forget that you get to play golf for a living. Most of us have work jobs that we don't really like. I would kill to have the opportunity that you have. Just go play and enjoy it – if not for yourself, for the rest of us who will never get the chance." I'm happy to report that Jason did find joy in the game again. I'm certainly not taking credit for that. It's just nice to see his jovial smile at tour events as often as possible.

As we covered on the 6th hole life and golf are just a series of moments that add up to a round, a tournament, a day, month, a life. Each and every moment offers the opportunity to be fully present and find joy no matter what is going on around us. So with golf it can be really as simple as hitting the best shot we can in the moment we are given to swing. At the end we add up our strokes, smile and shake hands with our playing partners. After all it's just a game - and games are meant to be fun.

With life it's not really any different. We go through a series of moments (one by one) and at the end we add up our score, except in this case our score doesn't really mean much. As the saying goes, 'you can't take it with you.' All the things a person can decide to worry about, he can decide to ignore. The pain of attachment will seem insignificant in the end. What matters most is the joy we experience and the love that we share.

I live in a world that is filled with divisiveness. I meet people who tell me they are miserable, tired, angry, and self-critical. I don't tell them what to do. I tell them what I'm going to do. I'm going to focus on what makes the world a good place. I'm going to pay attention to the beauty of diversity. I'm going to watch the birds soar only feet above the placid mirror of the water hazard. I'm going to give myself and everyone else a break, and I'm going to play golf. I'm going to play a lot of golf. And you are invited. Who's with me?

Ben Hogan once said, "As you walk down the fairway of life you must smell the roses, for you only get to play one round." Whether or not you believe in reincarnation, one thing remains undeniably true. We only get one shot at THIS life. Why not make it the best shot we're capable of?

Score	Explanation	Example
Eagle	You see life through the eyes of a giddy 3 year old.	Your life is like that scene in Singing in the Rain. Everything is awesome.
Birdie	You almost always choose joy.	Your cookie broke in half but now you have the chance to brighten the day of a stranger.
Par	To joy or not to joy. That is the question.	Should you be mad that you have to spend $6k to attend you're sister's wedding in Mauritius or happy for the chance to go somewhere exotic?
Bogey	Insignificant things cause you pain.	Ugh all these emails telling you how great your book is are so annoying because now you have to reply to them.
Double Bogey	You're miserable because life is so hard.	Your stupid job is making you go to 15 different countries in 3 months and you're gonna miss your daily Egg McMuffin and vanilla latte.

Score _____

Pro Tip

Always. Choose. Joy. It really is that simple. Make yourself aware that is your choice whether to have joy in your life not matter what is happening around you - and then make a good choice.

Practice Drills

◆ *Double Bogey* ◆ Lighten up and do something silly and child-like. Watch a children's movie that you really like, dance in the rain, or go to your favorite amusement park. It's time to stop taking things so seriously and look back to the days when you viewed the world with child-like wonder.

◆ *Bogey* ◆ Go out dancing with your friends. It doesn't matter if you are a good dancer or not. The point is to get on the dance floor and take part and, as they say, dance like no one is watching. You're not dancing for them anyway. You're dancing for you and your enjoyment. Who cares how you look? Just have fun!

◆ *Par* ◆ A great way to be more childlike is to be around kids while they are in fun environments. Consider volunteering for an after school program, coaching a youth sports team for kids under 10 or becoming a camp counselor at a kids summer camp.

The Scorer's Tent

At the end of a round it's a standard custom to go to the clubhouse bar to have a beer and some food while discussing the trials and tribulations that were just endured over the last four to five hours. It's a time for reflection and for tallying the final score. Let's do the same here and see how we did.

Hole 10 ★ Timing Is Everything – Learning not to force things.

Score _____

Hole 11 ★ Body of Work – Taking ownership of our health and well-being.

Score _____

Hole 12 ★ Jerk. Off. – Working on being a good person and setting good examples for others.

Score _____

Hole 13 ★ Intergi-tee – Being impeccable with your word and consistent with your actions.

Score _____

Hole 14 ★ Inclusivi-tee - Embracing diversity and using golf as a platform to teach acceptance of others.

Score _____

Hole 15 ★ Not So Great Expectations - Committing to the things we can control and letting go of those we cannot.

Score _____

Hole 16 ★ Critic's Choice – Learning to move past harsh self-criticism so you can do your best and find more enjoyment.

Score _____

Hole 17 ★ Lesson...the Pain – We never stop learning and growing as people and as golfers. Embrace the lesson so you can lessen the pain.

Score _____

Hole 18 ★ Enjoy the Journey – Learning to choose joy and make a life out of the moments that you are gifted.

Score _____

Front 9 Total Score To Par   _____

Back 9 Total Score To Par   _____

Total Overall Score To Par   _____

The 19th Hole

I hope you enjoyed reading this book nearly as much as I enjoyed writing it. It's meant to be a gift for those who want to uncover their best on or off of the golf course. I hope it helps.

Once again I would like to reiterate that because I have a good grasp on communicating the included points does not mean that I have everything figured out, or that I lead a perfect life. I am not a guru. If you've understood what I've written then you know that all of us are flawed in some way or another. The point is to be honest about our flaws and work on them as best we can. I am no different than you in that respect. I continue to work on myself and my game.

In this book, I wrote several passages about the world being a chaotic place filled with rage and divisiveness. I hope this book can be part of a community that focuses on creating a space for positivity and unity. I'm not under any illusions that this book is going to change the world. At the same time, if we all practice awareness and personally commit to being the best we can be, it could help. We cannot change the world, but we CAN change ourselves by focusing on the things that are within our control.

It's generally best to keep it simple. Rather than pointing out the flaws we find in others - to hide our own insecurities about our own flaws - we can choose to focus on ourselves. Or as Michael Jackson succinctly put it, 'start with the man in the mirror.' That's what makes golf the perfect vehicle to deliver these messages. It is a game that is best played when look-ing inward. It has taught me self-awareness and focus. It has taught me about what I can control - my swing, my thoughts, and my emotions.

If nothing else, I hope you had a good read and can shave a few strokes off your handicap. I thank you for your time and wish you well on your journey. Here's hoping that we all com-mit to bringing our best to the world!

> *"If I had to do it over again, I wouldn't*
> *beat myself up so much."*
> — *Gardner Dickinson*

Acknowledgements

Every person I have ever encountered has contributed in some way to helping me write this book, but don't worry I'm not going thank them all.

Everything I am and everything I've ever done was made possible through the unending love and support of my parents, Zaven and Janet Zildjian. They are simply the best guides, teachers, and friends that I could ever ask for. I can't imagine where I would be without them. Luckily I don't have to. My 3 siblings (Mark, Dianna, and Armen), their spouses (Alyson, Mike, and Sybil) and my 6 nieces and nephews have been an incredible extension of that family foundation that has provided eternal joy, love and laughter. All of you have always believed in me no matter what crazy ideas I have come up with and I am eternally grateful for each and every one of you.

Jason Ronstadt has been a good friend since our college days and I could never have dreamt of a more perfect editor with whom to take this wild ride. Without him, this would have been a long rambling essay with some interesting ideas. He helped me turn it into a book. Thanks for believing in Zilosophy to the point where you dragged Joe Marich into this. Joe is not only the best and most knowledgeable literary publicist/promotions guru, but he's also been an invaluable consultant on all levels of this project; his guidance has been truly priceless. As important, he has become a good friend and I look forward to many more zany literary and golfing adventures together.

Jason Gore is also a college buddy from Pepperdine. We've been friends since the mid-nineties and I've been the biggest fan of his career since he became a PGA player. When I first pitched him about the concept he said he loved it and agreed to write the foreword having read nothing. Thankfully for both of us, he was even more in love with the project after he did finally read the manuscript and I truly can't put into words what it has meant that he 'gets it' and is now using the book to try to be his best. His email explaining how on point the concept and execution was allowed me to release any remaining doubts that I had written a good book that might actually help golfers attain their best on and off of the course.

Matt Knabe and Matt Allard are two of the best friends I've ever had. I consider both to be brothers forever. Knabe is yet another college buddy and has been the most supportive friend I could imagine throughout the years. He too has always believed in my wacky ideas, whether he got them or not, and has been my greatest unofficial golf equipment sponsor for more than 20 years. Allard is my swing coach who by his patient yet assertive approach has allowed me to uncover my best swings, which has made the game of golf so much more enjoyable for me. He has also been the little brother I never had, and taught me so much more about life than he has about golf. The entire Knabe and Allard clans have taken me in as one of their own and I am truly blessed to be small a part of these amazing, golf-loving families.

I don't know where I'd be in my career, let alone in life without my brother from another mother, Kelly K. Most likely I would still be partying and drinking away my sorrows about being stuck in the music business. Kelly was the first person to ever ask me what I wanted my legacy to be. It is from that question that Zilosophy was eventually born. And the final catalyst of that birth was my brother from another dimension, Michael Brown. He woke me up to my gifts. He showed me that I could help people find their way through this wild human maze. I'm so blessed to have the friendship and mentorship that these two have provided.

There are several people who invested in this project, whose support helped turn it from a lofty dream into a reality. Thanks so much to Coach Chiodo, The Mental Dental, Lady Sybil and her Knight, j9 C., Joey Mulls, the Salty Manoogians and E-Z Bakery and Co. Special honorable mention goes to Baldwin Construction for hooking me up with a free beach house for 2 weeks where I wrote most of the first draft - a major initial step in realizing the concept.

I had a number of friends and family help with editing and general feedback throughout the writing process. Thank you all for your help, especially my favorite grammar enthusiast, Auntie Armenne. My good friend David Brody has been an incredible wealth of self-publishing knowledge and I'm thankful that all of my texts, calls and emails didn't scare him away.

There are 3 people that weren't directly involved with this project but whose friendships have meant so much to me over the years. Dino Malito, Janine Kerr and Matt Moss are family and I wouldn't be who I am without them.

As I said, there are too many others to list, but just know that if our paths have crossed, you have had an affect on me which has helped shape me into the person I am today. Thank you all for your contributions big or small.

Z Bio

Growing up in a small town outside of Boston, Michael Zildjian ("Z") never dreamt of being a writer. When he decided to move across the country to go to college at Pepperdine in Malibu, CA, a whole world opened up to him that he had never imagined. Talk about culture shock. Since then, he has traveled to 45 of the continental United States, and has dived head first into the cultures of a dozen or so international countries. He has met people from all walks of life, from rock stars to geologists, sharing his stories and his philosophical views about life while drinking adult beverages or playing a round of golf. And make no mistake; Z has played a lot of golf in a lot of places.

After moving on from careers as a concert promoter/producer, artist manager, licensing rep for TV/film, marketing/branding consultant, bartender, rideshare driver, and a disposable lighter repairman, to name just a few, Z decided it was time to take his passion for philosophical conversations to the next level. And thus Zilosophy was born. A place where Z could build a platform for public dialogue about the things he had always collaboratively pondered with friends, family and strangers.   Z is not a therapist, and he makes no professional therapeutic claims about his musings. He's just a dude you want to have a beer with in hopes you might get some needed perspective on life – or a good laugh. Or both.

Z now tours the U.S. and internationally speaking about Zilosophy at golf clubs, schools, corporate offices, barnyards, arcades and anywhere else people want to learn ways to bring their best to the golf course and beyond.

Please keep in touch. We love to hear your stories.
Visit us online at www.Zlosophy.org

Follow us on social media:

Facebook – www.facebook.com/Zilosophy

Instagram - @zilosophyongolf

Twitter - @yourpathforward

Zilosophy on Golf may be purchased for sale at your
pro shop, church fair or any place in between.
Please email info@zilosophy.org for more information.

Made in the USA
Middletown, DE
31 December 2019